THE MIRACLE BEFORE YOUR EYES

Patrick K. McAndrew

Library of Congress Control Number: 2017951755
ISBN-13:   Paperback: 978-1-64045-881-9
           PDF: 978-1-64045-882-6
           ePub: 978-1-64045-883-3
           Kindle: 978-1-64045-884-0
           Hardcover   978-1-64045-885-7

Printed in the United States of America

LitFire LLC
1-800-511-9787
www.litfirepublishing.com
order@litfirepublishing.com

The Miracle Before Your Eyes
by Patrick K. McAndrew
LitFire Publishing

Reviewed by Lee Ware

"One with Spirit, I remove the mask that hides the truth of who I am, and I experience the fullness of life!"

McAndrew gleams lessons from the stories of his own life and has turned them into pieces of inspiration and guidance for his readers. He begins with his turning point, a transition out of the restaurant industry after serving a man his final drink before he drove off and ended his life, which began his spiritual journey. Each story reads more like a sermon from a warm friend than a traditional story.

Often the story is anecdotal and sometimes he begins with an extended joke such as "a man walked into a restaurant with a full-grown ostrich walking beside him" and continues on for nearly two pages. It is as though one part is story—a narrative of the author's journey to discover himself—while another part is the wisdom gathered along the way subtly imparted as advice to anyone who needs it. Nothing reads forced nor preachy, but instead like when he describes going to ministry school as "a journey through a wilderness, filled with obstacles and challenges," but ultimately one of the most rewarding experiences of his life.

Each chapter begins with a nugget of sagacity that the reader is sure to hold onto, coming back to it over and over again. The quote serves as a lens through which to read the narrative, shedding light on its meaning. Repeating it at the end of each chapter is a nice touch and creates a sense of completion, a framework for each chapter.

While McAndrew's voice is conversational and often speaks directly to the reader, the words themselves are informed from many sources. In fact, each chapter lists the sources he drew knowledge and ideas from—ranging from The Holy Bible to Star Wars. McAndrew is clearly a student of human behavior and spirituality observing how humans "fail to listen to our inner knowing about the experiences in our life" and thus are doomed to relive our experiences over and over, sliding deeper into the darkness. But his book is a guide out of the darkness, and his observations are sure to stimulate and encourage his readers on their own paths of self-discovery.

I dedicate this book to my loving wife, Yvonne, who has been an inspiration and a support as we have walked this path called life. She has been with me through the ups and downs every step of the way.

I would also like to dedicate it to my amazing daughter, Shavonne, who is talented, understanding and wise beyond her years.

And to all my teachers and mentors I have had along the way, especially Mike and Sara Matoin and Sallye Taylor

I would also like to say thank you to all those who tried to help me with their editing skills especially; Christy Cooper, Joann Gardner, Stanley Maness, John O'Leary and the staff at FriesenPress. I have much appreciation for you.

Table of Contents

Foreword

Hello my friend,

Life is a miracle, and the journey that has helped me to realize this has been incredible. The journey of awakening has taken me from one of the lowest points in my life to moments of extraordinary realizations and revelations. Some of these experiences have been remarkable, and some may be hard to believe. The process of awakening and healing has given me the ability to see a much more encompassing view of the world than I ever thought possible.

Life continually unfolds and changes, showing us new dimensions. As we move through challenging situations, a ripple will occasionally appear in the fabric of life, where none existed before, and we are able to notice and sense things we have never encountered before. It can be compared to stopping and looking at a flower. We may have seen it bud, and then blossom. However, it's not until we study its petals that we can see its uniqueness and the qualities it possesses.

Likewise, it is not until we pause and study a segment of life that we realize its complexities, its depths, and its wonder. This was actually something my grandfather taught me quite by accident. I greatly loved and admired my grandfather and he was a very special influence in my life. However, it was not until his funeral that I heard some of the incredible stories of his life, of his unselfish love, and the sacrifices he had made. These incredible stories revealed the extraordinary life my grandfather had lived, and highlighted the positive impact he had on many people.

It was not until his friends and loved ones had paused to reflect upon his life—and the unique qualities he had—that the miracle that had been his life was made clear to me. I also realized that we all have unique stories that might inspire and help others on their own journeys.

When I became conscious of being on a journey of awakening, the lesson I had learned from my grandfather's life became very valuable. I had learned that every challenge, every difficulty, every situation we find ourselves in can provide us with insights—into our own experiences—that are necessary for our soul's unfoldment. So I learned to pause, reflect, and contemplate what was happening in my life, to see what message was hidden within any experience. I would ask myself, "What are the forces that have led me to this point? What do I have to learn from this experience? How could I have done this differently? I began to study the situations and events I found myself in, see my own stories unfolding before my eyes, and realize the messages hidden deep within them.

Whenever I have shared my personal stories, and the insights I have gained from them, I have found they have engaged the imagination of the listeners. People have often responded, "Wow, you should tell that story in a book." Over the past twenty years, one of the things I have learned to do is follow the promptings and the inner nudges I receive. Although I must say, in the case of writing and creating this book, those inner nudges were really more of a nagging feeling that would not go away.

These nudges told me I needed to share my personal stories, and my insights about them, with a much larger audience. They were important to pass on, and could be meaningful to others who have had similar challenges. Often when we are able to look at our life—or someone else's—with understanding, we can unlock the deeper mysteries of life that often bewilder us. It's as if an invisible veil just falls away and we suddenly see the matter clearly. As I have contemplated my personal experiences, I found that they have been great learning tools for me; and when I share these experiences with others, they help them to gain a much broader perspective of life. It is my hope that this book will do the same for you.

Therefore, I invite you to read the contents of this book with an open mind; perhaps even treat it as something simply to stretch your thinking. Actually, it is my hope that you can read the book as an adventure, for indeed it has been an adventure of exploration and growth. Most of the stories enclosed are my own adventures, often taken with my wife and daughter. If you look closely enough, you may even be reminded of some of your own experiences.

So, join me in the adventure; you might hope with me, laugh with me, cry with me, and be inspired with me. As you read, if there is anything that you do not understand or agree with, please set aside your questions and doubts—for the time being—and just allow your mind to soar on the possibilities. Remember, these are stories, lessons, and insights revealed through the exploration and by searching for a deeper meaning in the chaos we call "life."

Perhaps, like they did with me, they will help you to see the miracle before your eyes.

Turning Point

I behold the miracle before me eyes

I remember the day it happened—the day my journey of awakening began. I had been struggling with my work in the restaurant industry, where I had been employed for 21 years. Food service is a gift that comes naturally for me, but it's a career filled with crazy 80-hour workweeks and many angry people. My bosses were demanding and yelled a lot. They paid little attention to the success the business found, or the time their mangers and employees invested. They shared very little encouragement. It was like working with the Chef from *Hell's Kitchen*. It felt demeaning, and I had lost my passion for the work!

One of my joys was helping our customers, which is actually where my journey of awakening began. Late one night, near closing, my bartender disappeared into the back to fetch a few needed items. John, a long time customer, called me over and asked to have his nightcap: Jack Daniels on the rocks. That was easy enough, so I jumped behind the bar, poured the drink, talked with him for a few minutes, and then returned to the front desk. A little later—as I was standing at the door—he bid me goodnight, walked out, got into his new big, green, mean machine and sped away, peeling out into the street. Just after his car left my sight, I heard the screeching of tires, and then the thunderous sound of shattering glass, and bending metal. John had run a red light and was broadsided by another vehicle. He died instantly.

That was it! I was overwhelmed by the news of his death. I felt, and believed, I was partially responsible. This event, combined with the emotional state I was already in due to the nature of my work environment, made it very hard living with my self. I had a melt down. I couldn't deal with the restaurant industry any longer, so the next morning I quit my job, and the industry! I had no idea what I was going to do. I had a college degree, but restaurant work was really the only "work" I knew anything about. What was I going to do? How was I going to live with myself?

After sitting for a few days, in the solitude of my condo, I decided I needed to get out and do something. A few hours later, I found myself sitting on the beach of a small lake, near where I lived. As I sat by the shore of the lake, I marveled at what a beautiful summer day it was. It had been a long time since I had just sat like that, in the quiet of a beautiful day. It was in the mid 80's, under clear blue skies, with northern geese swimming not too far away. It was beautiful, calm, and serene—everything my life was not. I missed my old life in Virginia, where I had been raised, and being able to walk in the beauty of the Blue Ridge Mountains, or along the shore of the ocean, whenever I felt their call. They were far away, not just in my physical reality, but in how now I experienced life and the wonder of nature.

As I sat alone at the shore of that small lake, I breathed in the fresh air, closed my eyes, and said, "Oh God what am I going to do? Please help me! What is life supposed to be like? What am I to do? How can I experience the things I hold dear, especially when my heart hurts so badly? God, please help me." Then I just breathed, and waited with my eyes closed. In my mind, I could somehow see the grass and the lake that surrounded me. Then my vision moved deeper, as if I could see *inside* the blades of grass, the lake, the trees, and the geese; I could see them at a cellular level. I didn't really understand it at the time, but I could see them all breathing in this *glowing, vibrating energy*, even the chlorophyll in the cells of grass and trees. I could see them all breathing in this glowing vibrating energy.

Then I looked within myself, and I could see that *glowing, vibrating energy* moving in me, in my lungs and my heart, and the blood coursing through my veins. Then I realized a moment of oneness with all the life that surrounded me; it was that *glowing, vibrating energy* that somehow tied us all together.

I had no idea what really was happening; I had no concept of the spiritual dimension or its disciplines: meditation, visualization and prayer. But, I did realize that something extraordinary was happening! I was experiencing a miracle of life that had always been there—right there before my eyes—even though I had never seen "It" or experienced anything like "It" before.

It was then I realized what I loved the most about the mountains and the ocean of Virginia where I had grown up: the inner beauty I felt when I looked at them; the peacefulness; the serenity; the unrealized presence of this *glowing, vibrating energy* I could feel within me. I had been projecting them onto the mountains and the ocean, and what I could see "out there."

These two back-to-back experiences served as a turning point in my life, which opened me to whole new way of being. The night at the bar was the 2X4 experience—, an event that hits you right upside the head—that caused me to let go of what I clung so tightly onto, so I could open up to what was about to flow in: my mystical experience by the lake. Perhaps you have heard the saying, "When you get to your wit's end, you will find God lives there." That's what happened to me.

A few weeks later, I really surprised my wife by going to church with her, which is something we had never done together in our five years of marriage, and something I had not done in eighteen years. This church turned out to be a place that would help me to realize my soul's desire to experience more and more of the divine wonders that surround us each moment of each day.

Years later, I came across the words of Pelagious, a fourth century Celtic monk, and the memories of my turning point came to life. Pelagious taught that a narrow shaft of divine light shines down from on high, to pierce the veil that separates Heaven from earth. It is in these narrow shafts that God can be glimpsed moving in life. Pelagious wrote, "Look at the animals roaming the forest; God's Spirit dwells in them. Look at the birds flying across the sky; God's Spirit dwells within them. Look at the tiny insects crawling in the grass; God's Spirit dwells in them ... It was not only that His hands had fashioned every creature; it was that

'His breath' had brought every creature to life ... The presence of God's Spirit is in all living things and is what makes them beautiful." [1]

These words also caused a flood of other memories to come pouring into my mind. I thought of the day my daughter was born, when I felt God's presence in the room. I thought of several months earlier when I went with my wife, Yvonne, to see her first sonogram, and the very first time I heard my daughter's heartbeat. I was overwhelmed; as I listened closely, I could hear the heartbeat of God within her heartbeat.

I don't know about you, but whenever I pick up a newborn, I see God's life stirring in its pureness—a radiant presence and a pure knowing. I see a miracle before my eyes.

I believe we were all born with this same original virtue—born in the image and likeness of our Creator. Yes, I was born; you were born; we were born in original virtue, created in the image and likeness of God! At least that's what it says in the Bible (Genesis 1:27).

That image and likeness is not the fleshly body suits we wear, but "the Breath of Life God breathed into us as living beings," as Pelagious wrote about. The Breath of God *is* that glowing, vibrating energy I saw at the lake that day. God is the Sacred Breath of life, of wisdom, of love, of creativity, and oh so much more!

According to the words of Jesus, and the story of Adam's creation in the second chapter of Genesis, I believe this image and likeness of God *is* "Spirit. Remember Jesus' words, in the Gospel of John, as he spoke to the woman at the well. He said, "God is Spirit, and those who worship God will do so in Spirit and Truth." (John 4:24) The word translated as "Spirit"—"Spiritus," in Latin, Greek, and Aramaic—actually means "breath," and refers to the breath of life. The breath of life is glowing, vibrating, sacred energy that fills us each moment. God, in this moment, is breathing out the universe, and giving expression to everything in it, including you and I.

There are many miracles that can be experienced through our partaking in this breath of life. One miracle is the way God tries to communicate with us, through the gift of hearing. I find it to be an extraordinary gift, because I can hear well beyond the range of most people. When I go into

---

1 Listening for the Heartbeat of God, A Celtic Spirituality, J. Philip Newell, Paulist Press, New York, NY and Mahwah, NJ, page 10

a restaurant, I can hear the conversations of people two and three tables away. My wife tells me my good hearing is really just selective hearing, and that I select to listen to the conversations I'm not supposed to be listening to, as opposed to the conversation I am suppose to be listening to. Do you think she is trying to tell me something?

Yes, my extraordinary hearing is a miracle; although sometimes I think it is a curse, like: when I pick the wrong conversation to listen to; when a motorcycle rumbles down the street; or when the emergency test sirens, which are right behind my house, go off. It can be a little trying on my nerves.

Then, there are other times I know it's a blessing. Sometimes, when it is really still and quiet, it's as if I can hear the universe moving all about me, playing within my heart and soul. Now I know you are probably thinking, "Wow, are you crazy, man! You might have good hearing, but no way can you hear the universe moving. The universe does not make any sounds. That is just nonsense!"

But is it? Are you sure?

There is a space flight documentary that shows how, after the engines are cut and the sound of the spacecraft removed, a kind of buzz or OMMMM can be heard in the background, like soft music playing somewhere beneath the silence. What is the source of this sound? The scientists have no idea, do you? I believe it is the heartbeat of the universe—a perfect resonance within space. It is God chanting.

When studied closely, it has been found that all of life has it's own unique sound; you might even call it a frequency. Each species has its own unique vibration rate. As the cells work in our bodies, they send an energy vibration out into the world. As the different vibration rates blend together, a rhythm or beat can be heard underlying all life. If you listen closely, you can hear the sounds of life vibrating silently within your heart; however, to hear it you have to know the sound is there, and awaken to its presence.

Have you heard the flutter of a butterfly's wings, a flower dancing in the wind, a kitten purr? These are all sounds that help to create the heartbeat of the universe. You have to listen closely to hear them. If you don't, *true life* will pass you by.

Yes, all of life has a quiet beat to it. It can be seen, felt, and sensed, but to do so, we have to stop, take a break from all our bus-e-ness. I am sure you have heard water flowing in a country stream, rain falling, and the sound of thunder at night. Can you remember lying in the grass, while feeling and smelling its scent, as the wind blew across your face? When you reconnect with these moments, you will recall hearing, sensing, and feeling the heartbeat of life.

I think one thing that draws people to the ocean is the feeling they get when they watch and listen to the waves rumbling ashore. The constant motion has a kind of hypnotic trance to it. Within the ocean's simple movements, you can hear the heartbeat of the universe. When I walked the deserted winter beaches of Virginia, I felt the ocean's heartbeat in its movements. It produced a feeling of complete oneness and peace.

During warmer times, many first time visitors to the ocean are caught in its hypnotic trance. They do not realize the power of the waves, so as they approach, they stand tall. The wave crashes into them and knocks them down. Sometimes, waves pours over them with such might the current pushes them all the way to shore. Those who approach the wave in this manner are at the mercy of the wave.

Most swimmers do not let the force of the waves dissuade them. They try and try again, challenging the waves, achieving the same results until they realize there is a better way. Finally, they accept the fact that the wave is more powerful than they are, and discover a different way to deal with it. They become One with the water, by diving under it.

Life for us is no different. We can stand tall in the face of the Force of Life, resisting the current, struggling to keep our heads above water, or we can acknowledge it. Acknowledging there is a greater power in life is simply an admission of an obvious fact. Only then can we begin to open up and become one with nature and the heartbeat of life.

One of my favorite things to do at the beach is body surfing. You swim out to a point in the surf where the waves are just beginning to break, and then you wait for just the right wave. You can literally feel the heartbeat of the water, as the swell of the waves begins to pull and lift you at the same time. When you feel the pull of the water is just right, you begin to swim. If you have timed the wave right, you quickly pick up speed, and can allow the wave to carry you all the way to the shore, in a rush of energy. I have had waves carry me more than fifty yards in just a few seconds; it is exhilarating.

However, if you do not align yourself with the wave in just the right way, if you struggle or fight against the wave, you are left behind. Likewise, when we place ourselves in alignment with the Force of Life it can be exhilarating, as it carries us to new places, and gives us insight and experiences we have only dreamed. One of the neat things about body surfing, as it is with life, is that you will always be offered a chance to catch the next wave.

When Jesus was asked when the Kingdom of God would come, he replied, "The Kingdom of God is not coming in things to be observed; they will not say, 'Look here it is or there it is!' For in fact the Kingdom of God is in the midst of you" (Luke 17:20). The Kingdom of God (Heaven) is the heartbeat of life and the miracle before our eyes, but we have to open our inner "I" to see it. When we do, this Kingdom of goodness will reveal itself in a variety of ways and dimensions. Jesus did say, "In our father's house there are many mansions..." Why then would we expect there to be only one.

I have mentioned just a few of the mystical experiences I have had on my journey of awakening, to the miracles before our eyes—experiences shared with me through my physical senses of sight, sound, and feeling, when I opened up and became aware of Spirit's Presence. I would like to invite you to join me on the incredible journey of awakening. If you might be so bold and willing to do so, I have a few tasks for you to undertake before you read the next chapter.

First, make a commitment to notice the miracle before your eyes. Often we get so caught up in living life with all its bus - e - ness, worries, and anxieties about things we think are wrong, that we fail to realize what is right ... and that life, in and of itself, is a miracle. Life is a miracle and can be seen everywhere we look. It is in the wind moving through the trees. It is in the blossoming of a flower. It can be seen in a snow-covered mountain, the ripples of the ocean tides, and in the magnificence of the rising sun. It can be experienced in the purr of a kitten or the roar of a lion. The fact that you are breathing—that oxygen is filling your lungs, that you are reading these words, that you can see around the room, and experience the life that fills it—is a miracle! Take the time to notice it!

Second, start each day by looking into the mirror and saying, "Good morning self, you are a miracle and this is going to be a miraculous day."

Third, I would like you to close your eyes and say, "I am a miracle." Then see yourself being immersed in the glowing, vibrating, sacred energy. See It permeating every cell of your being. Then, if you dare, visualize what the inside of your body looks like—your heart, your cells. See the glowing, vibrating energy flowing in you, and say it once more, "I am a miracle. The life that flows through me, as me, is a miracle. Thank you God, for the miracle of life that is me!"

As you let go of all that holds you back, you will discover life is a miracle, an ever-expanding field of possibilities and of goodness! Then, in small increments, you will discover how to harness its tremendous potential. You will learn that you do not have to just stand in the face of the waves of life, allowing them to crash over you. You can swim a little further on the ocean of life, where you can feel the heartbeat of true life, and allow Its swell to lift you, so that you can ride the surge all the way to the shores of your dreams.

I behold the miracle before my eyes!

Resources for this Chapter:

- Listening for the Heartbeat of God, A Celtic Spirituality, J. Philip Newell, Paulist Press, New York, NY and Mahwah, NJ

- What Are You? Imelda Shanklin, Unity Books, Unity Village MO

- The Handbook of Positive Prayer, Hypathia Hasbrouck, Unity Books, Unity Village, MO

- The Holy Bible, New Revised Standard Version.

Instinct

I Am the Light of the world, and I allow my Light to shine!

Once upon a time, a Sunday school teacher asked her group of children if anyone could quote the Twenty-third Psalm. One cute, four-and-a-half-year-old girl raised her hand. A bit impressed, the teacher inquired if she could really say the whole psalm. The little girl stood up, smiled, and said, "The Lord is my shepherd; that's all I want." She then bowed and sat down.[2]

What a wonderful interpretation! It certainly speaks to the spiritual wisdom of children, and to our most basic instinct of all, which is to know the infinite creative force within all life.

Ever since I was a teenager, I have had a reoccurring dream, which would often come into my conscious mind. The first part of this dream is as a young boy, and I am walking along a trail that runs through a deep forest. As the trail curves, I have an impulse to cut through some thick underbrush. After making my way through the underbrush, I look up and find I am standing by a large, turbulent river. It is flowing westward towards the ocean and the setting sun. The river bends around the point of land on which I am standing, from a gorge that must be at least two hundred feet deep. As I look at the turbulent waters, shooting out of the gorge towards me, I see large salmon jumping out of the water, fighting their way to make it upstream. The view is breathtaking. I catch myself deep in thought: "Why do the salmon struggle so hard against the current? Why are they not content to swim where they are? The water is deep; there is plenty of food, and the scenery is beautiful. Why do they fight so hard to swim upstream?"

As I contemplate the meaning of this vision, another memory enters my mind, and I find myself looking out across the northern plains. I am standing on the shore of a large lake; a flock of geese soars over my head, and then dive towards the lake, skimming across the surface before coming to a gentle landing atop the water. Looking around, I see hundreds, no … *thousands* of geese. They are all talking to each other—cackling and quacking. It is an amazing site. I ask myself, "Why have they come here to this place? Where have they come from?"

As I consider this thought, my mind goes deeper into contemplation, and a final memory forges its way into my mind. It is as though I am transported back in time more than a hundred years. I find myself standing on the western plains, where hundreds of buffalo roam! These huge creatures are grazing, as far as I can see over the top of a hill and beyond. Then, in one moment, they look up and begin to run; soon they are gone from sight. Where did they go? Why did they leave? Why were they not content to stay here and graze on these Great Plains?

All life follows its own unique and innate instinct. All of creation follows a set process of birth, growth, procreation, maturing, and then passing onto a new realm. All the species of creation have a divine plan, and follow their natural instinct for life. Salmon in the Pacific Northwest swim from the deep waters of the ocean to the shallow waters of local rivers upstream, to give birth before they die. The great northern geese fly hundreds of miles north each summer, to mate and give birth to their young before returning south. The monarch butterfly and the hummingbird, such tiny creatures, fly from southern Mexico, to points north and east in the United States and Canada. Bears and many other animals hibernate during the cold of winter. All of life follows its own natural instinct, as the divine plan for their life unfolds. They follow this natural, inner calling, despite the consequences of the struggle, for it is who they are! You never hear a tree complaining about where it was planted, nor does a butterfly question the length of its flight, nor fear the obstacles that lie on its path.

As I reflect on these memories, I am often left in contemplation of my own life, wondering, "What is my natural instinct? Why am I here? Why are we here? What is mankind's most basic instinct? Survival, love ... what?"

Some people would have you believe that man is prone to violence, and that our innate instinct is to do evil. They point to the story of Adam and Eve, eating that apple in the Garden of Eden. Many will tell you, in that moment, mankind fell from God's grace, and that it has become man's most basic nature to listen to that snake, which they have called Satan and the Devil.

Based on many of the things we see on television and read in newspapers, we might conclude that this evil instinct appears to be true, and reinforces what I believe is erroneous thinking. Appearances can be deceiving, which is only one of the many challenges we face. As a result of biting into a piece of delicious looking fruit, which came from "the tree of the knowledge of good and evil," we gained the tendency to judge things through the filters and perceptions of our mortal minds.

The fact is that nowhere in that story, found in the second and third chapters of Genesis, is there any mention of the Devil, Satan, or evil. It was just Adam, Eve, a rather opinionated and persuasive snake, and God. Nor is there any other mention of those characters in the book of Genesis. They do not appear anywhere in the Bible until the Books of Chronicles and Job, which chronologically are twelve books and many years later. Somewhere along the way, the concept of the devil started being used as a unique way for people to shirk their responsibilities. The phrase "The devil made me do it," was created as a way of saying, "I do not want to take responsibility for my words, decisions, actions, or creations."

I think it is odd that some theologies have cast into darkness the very powerful insights that can be gained by studying the stories about the Garden of Eden. They do this through the teachings of original sin and man's fall from grace. This shifts the responsibility for our decisions and actions onto another entity that somehow would, and could, steal our souls from an all-powerful, all-knowing God. They blame mankind's fall from God's grace squarely on Eve's shoulders—Eve and that sneaky little snake. We all know the story! Well now, is that really what happened? Would the Loving Father, and the Creator of the entire universe, condemn all of mankind for eternity as a result of one person's desire to bite into a tasty-looking piece of fruit?

I don't know about you, but I think that is being just a little bit obsessive-compulsive. Now, would an all powerful, all knowing God be so obsessive-compulsive? Would It allow some dark force to steal your soul? That does not sound very logical to me!

The concept of original sin has had a very negative impact on western society and the way we think, especially when seen through the eyes of Constantine's Church. This warped 17th century theological interpretation of the very powerful story of mankind's creation, is actually at the root of what we find to be most challenging part of life in the 21st century; it is also at the root of much of the darkness in the world, causing fear, anxiety, and separation, and leaving us to wonder, "Am I good enough? Am I worthy?"

Anyone who studies human behavior knows that when human beings are put to the test, we are capable of extraordinary feats of love and compassion. We also know that the desire to experience love and to do God's will have been underlying motivates for some of the most horrendous acts. Unfortunately, our loving nature is often covered over by our hurts, pains, and fears. Our most basic instinct has been hidden by the processes of learning the ways of the physical world, and by the darkness many us have been taught exists through the teachings of original sin.

Quite paradoxically, you will find, at the roots of most of the world's cultures, the belief that light was one of the creative forces of the universe. Even the Genesis account of creation is built upon the theory that the primordial substance of the universe is light, although it tends to be overlooked when discussing man's most basic instinct. This creation story foretold a modern day concept, with which many scientists agree, that the most basic element of all matter is the photon—an infinitesimally small fleck of light. Many ancient cultures worshiped the sun as God—as the Creator and giver of life. In Egypt, Pharaoh was the sun God incarnate. In Persia, Mithra was worshiped as the incarnation of eternal light. Ancient cultures around the world held festivals to celebrate the winter solstice, during the last weeks of December, when daylight hours are shortest and the amount of sunlight begins to increase each day. Greece, Italy, the Scandinavian countries of Norway and Sweden, the ancient Druids of Ireland and Scotland, the Hindu and Buddhist countries of the Far East, even the Inca and Mayan peoples of Central America celebrated the winter solstice. The winter solstice festivals were held to celebrate the increase of daylight, the triumph of the light over darkness.

Please note that the term "light" has been used as a recurring symbol for Spirit, divine intelligence, and wisdom. God is considered to be the primordial light. Jesus is said to be an archetype for the higher self, echoing the words found in the Gospel of John: "The true light that enlightens" everyone. Jesus told his followers to let their light shine, to let their true selves—the image of God they were created to be—to express into their world.

There is an ancient Gnostic story about the beginning of time, which I heard many years ago. The Gnostics were a diverse group of philosophers, who believed that all knowledge in the universe flowed forth from a place of light deep within us, which could be drawn forth to spark personal insights and revelations. The story had the ring of truth to it, and it provoked my imagination in such a way that I can easily recall it. I believe this story focuses on what I believe to be man's most basic instinct.

66

In the beginning God, the Creator, created the universe, filling it with many wonders. He also gave life to other creative beings like Himself, so that He would have someone to share the awesome delights of His universe. One of these creative beings was named Sophia; she was the goddess of beauty and light. Sophia was so moved by the Creator's grand gesture, she wanted to do something in return to show her gratitude. She thought long and hard about what to do, and finally she had an idea. The idea sprang to life, a living spectrum of light and beauty, which stretched across the universe. It was a breathtaking sight; its radiance was something to behold. The Spectrum of Light and Life knew who it was and knew its purpose was to be One with the Spectrum of Light and Life that stretched across the universe, and to reflect the life, light, and beauty of the Creator.

Another creative being, by the name of Darth, saw Sophia's marvelous creation, wondered how he could ever create anything that would compare with it, and became jealous. In a fit of rage, Darth smashed The Spectrum of Light and Life into millions of pieces. However, when the fragments of light and life reached the corners of the universe, a very strange thing happened. The pieces of light and life began to draw back together, for they knew who they were. They knew their purpose was to be one with The Spectrum of Light and Life, to reflect the life, light, and beauty of the Creator. Soon, The Spectrum of Light and Life once again stretched across the galaxies, shining as brilliantly as before.

Darth watched in dismay, and realized he needed to come up with a better plan. Darth plotted and planned in secret, until he came up with what he thought was a perfect plan. He designed a series of planets and moons that revolved around a single star. He gave the planet an atmosphere and gravity to hold solid objects in place. Then, he molded millions of little clay capsules.

When everything was ready, Darth moved towards the Spectrum of Light and Life once again, and shattered it into millions of pieces. The fragments of light fell to the planets that circled the star. As they did, Darth enclosed the fragments of light in the capsules of clay. The clay capsules sprang to life from the energy of those fragments of light, which they now enclosed. As long as the clay enclosed the fragments of light, they forgot that they were beings of Light and Life, and they forgot that their purpose was to be one with the Spectrum of Light and Life. However, the clay figures felt unexplained urges and longings to experience more of life. They knew little of how to fulfill those longings, because the clay figures did not know they were really beings of Light and Life, nor that their purpose was to be one with the Spectrum of Light and Life.

After some time, the clay figures began to wear out, and holes developed, and the beings of light and life were able to escape from the capsules. As they did, they remembered who they were and began to return to be one with the Spectrum of Light and Life. Darth became very concerned about this, because he realized that it would not be long before the entire the Spectrum of Light and Life would once more stretch across the universe.

So, he developed a new plan. Each time a clay figure developed a leak, through which the inner being of Light and Life could escape, he was there with a new suit of clay, to catch it before it could return to be one with The Spectrum of Light and Life, to which it longed to return.

As the story goes, the beings of Light and Life, enclosed in the bodies of clay, began to slowly awaken to the urges and longings that called to them from the depth of their being. They began to realize they were much more than they appeared to be. They realized the truth of who they were. They realized that they were beings of Light and Life with special powers and that their purpose, their longing, was to reflect the light, life and beauty of the Creator –to one day return to be one with the Spectrum of Light and Life.

—————————————————————— 99 ——————————————————————

Interesting story, is it not? Does any of it have a familiar ring to you? We are those beings of light and life. Our deepest longing, our most basic instinct, is to reach out and be one with the infinite Spectrum of Light and Life to reflect the light, life, and beauty of the Creator. We experience this longing of our soul in many different ways, but often it is misunderstood. We experience it as a feeling of lack or loneliness. We try to fill the emptiness we feel by acquiring things, by over-eating, by taking drugs or drinking alcohol. We seek to fill the longing by claiming power and control over others, or by living on the extremes of our physical reality. However, we will never satisfy the longings of our soul until we turn our attention inward, remembering to reflect the life, light, and beauty of God's presence.

I think it is amazing that Jesus repeated this advice over and over again, but because people have been so focused on their outer condition, they never understood the meaning of his words. He said, "The Kingdom of Heaven is at hand," – it is here now; turn back to God, and hear the good news (Mark 1:15). He said, "The Kingdom of God is in the midst of you." (Luke 17:20) Jesus is pointing out that the way to satisfy that longing of our souls is by knowing God within our hearts.

The Truth is, God is the way to experience the deepest longings of our hearts. Just as the four-year-old girl in the opening story said, "The Lord is my Shepherd; that's all I want." We are beings of Light and Life, and our most basic instinct is to be one with the Infinite Spectrum of Light and Life, which is God. God is the way, the truth, and the light of our being. Reach out with your inner awareness, listen to the longings of your heart, and know that the Infinite One loves you.

I Am the Light of the world, and I allow my Light to shine!

Resources for this Chapter

- *Lesson Notes of Christopher Chenowethe,* www.positivechristianity.org

- Sacred Myths, Marilyn McFarlane, Sibyl Publications, Portland, OR

- *Mysteries of Genesis,* Charles Fillmore, Unity Books, Unity Village, MO

- *The Holy Bible, New Revised Standard Version*

"The Mask" -- A Veil of Darkness

One with Spirit, I remove the mask that hides the truth of who I am,
and I experience the fullness of life!

One Sunday morning, a woman got up early and took a long walk. Afterward, she decided to treat herself to a double-dip, chocolate ice cream cone. She hopped in the car, and drove over to a bakery and ice cream parlor. When she went in, there was only one other customer in the store: Paul Newman! He was sitting at the counter having a doughnut and coffee, and looking gorgeous as usual. The woman's heart skipped a beat, as her eyes made contact with those famous baby-blue eyes. The actor nodded graciously, and the star-struck woman smiled demurely.

"Pull yourself together!" she thought to herself. "You are a happily married woman with three children; you are forty-five years old, not a teenager!" The clerk filled her order, and she took the double-dip, chocolate ice cream cone in one hand and her change in the other. Then, she went out the door, avoiding even a glance in Paul Newman's direction.

When she reached her car, she realized that she had a handful of change, but her other hand was empty. "Oh, no! Where's my ice cream cone? Did I leave it in the store?" Back into the shop she went, expecting to see the cone still in the clerk's hand or in a holder on the counter, or something. But, there was no ice cream cone anywhere in sight. With confusion, she happened to look over in Paul Newman's direction. His face broke into his familiar warm, friendly smile as he said to her, "You put it in your purse." .

Sometimes we do forget ourselves, do we not?

Recently, while waiting to meet someone at the airport, I was left with some time on my hands simply to observe the people passing by, which is one of the things I love to do. There was a young woman pushing a stroller down the concourse. She stopped at a nearby phone to make a call. In the stroller, there was a baby boy, about a year and half old; he had red hair and bright blue eyes. He looked straight into my eyes with a child's gaze. A natural and beautiful sense of peace filled me. I could see the excitement in his eyes, as he seemed to sense something: "A big person who knows who he is!"

Sometimes, I think young children view adults just as big people walking around in a trance, not remembering who they truly are. The look the child extended me said, "I know who you are! You are my friend, God's perfect child, the Christ." He started to play with the phone cord, while his mother talked on the phone unaware of our silent conversation. The child looked up at me again, as if to say, "Life really is exciting." Then, he went back to amusing himself with the phone cord. I thought, "Isn't life a wonder." When the mother finished her call, she walked away, pushing the stroller, with the red-headed toddler leaning out around the back of the stroller, to sneak one more glimpse at me before they were gone; and, I was left alone to contemplate the experience.

Children certainly are a marvel. They are filled with curiosity and love. They have no fear and so much energy. If only we could tap into their energy. How do they do it? However, there are times when their energy gets on our nerves. That is nothing new; it has been happening for centuries. Even during Jesus' time, we find that children were a challenge to some adults. In the 18th chapter of Luke, people were trying to bring their children to Jesus, and the disciples stopped them. Jesus, seeing this, reprimanded the disciples, saying, "Do not hold the children back, for whoever does not receive the Kingdom of God like a child shall not enter." Then, he took the children into his arms.

Why do you think Jesus said that? What could he have meant by this demonstration? What can we learn from children? How can we become, "like a child"? Children live life in the moment, and experience life one moment at a time. They do not wear "the mask" to hide their feelings, or the bright inner radiance of God's Spirit. Their faces glow when they are happy and filled with joy. Their intuition is remarkably clear, and they have a natural knowledge of Spirit that can be incredible, if they are encouraged and allowed to express it. When children get mad, they let us know it right away. They do not hold it back. They let us know just how upset they are with their tantrums and the slamming of doors. They feel their feelings in the moment, as they move through the experience, and then it is over. When they are done, they are off to something else in a very short time. In comparison, adults have learned to wear the mask of approval, while holding their feelings in and holding onto a grudge for years. In order for us to experience the wholeness of life, we must remove the mask, trusting in God, which will allow us to live life fully in the moment, just as a child.

I have a marvelous teacher, who is a product of God's grace and love. She has taught me much about what it is to be a child of God, and about my true identity and purpose. She is my daughter, Shavonne. She has shown me, beyond any doubt, that we are all born into this world with our spiritual identity and purpose intact, that we are radiant beings of light, totally aware of God's life. She has taught me that we are spiritual beings who have been cloaked with garments of skins (Genesis 3:20). Infants and young children are in their truest nature closest to God. When you look into their eyes, you can see their incredible Spirit. Generally, small children see life as good. They maintain a certain level of innocence. They are loved and their needs are met.

As infants, we already have within us all the knowledge we need to understand the spiritual dimension of life. Remembering this knowledge is simply a matter of being able to draw the information out of us, through our intuition. One grandmother told me of a time when her three-year-old grandson sat on the floor, watching and listening to her struggle over a decision that she had to make. The grandson finally stopped her, saying, "Grandma, it's okay; it's okay. Do not worry. The answer is in your heart. You only have to listen."

Another example of this inner wisdom that children possess, happened when my family and I were living in Kansas City. Shavonne was about three years old. She was lying on the floor, engrossed in her coloring book, with everything spread out around her. Seeing her lying there, Yvonne—my wife—was prompted to ask, "Shavonne, what is freedom?" Shavonne, without looking up, answered immediately: "Understanding."

Yvonne, in awe at the pure wisdom of her statement, wanted to verify what Shavonne meant by that answer, so she asked, "What do you mean, understanding?" Shavonne replied, "Don't you know, Mama? Understand God, and you understand everything, and that's freedom." Yvonne was flabbergasted. Meanwhile, our daughter never looked up or skipped a beat in her coloring. It is through the wisdom, flowing out of the mouth of babes, that we know the awesome power and intelligence that lies buried within us all. That is, if we take the time to listen!

Children start out being so honest with their thoughts and feelings. Unfortunately, it is we adults who change them. Children speak their minds, often to our embarrassment. "Grandpa, how come you always smell like moth balls?"

How about something my daughter said, when she was seven: "Mom, are you pregnant?" My wife answered, "No dear, I have just put on a few pounds." Shavonne then said, "Are you sure you don't have a baby in there; it sure looks like it." Yvonne turned to me, and said, "It's time to lose some weight." Perhaps you have heard the story of the five year old, who was caught sneaking into his baby brother's room. While peering over the crib, he asked the infant, "Tell me about God, I'm beginning to forget."

As children grow, they begin to learn "the ways of the world" and, consequently, begin to forget their spiritual nature. They learn the ways of the world by what they are taught by their role models—either intentionally, or unintentionally. Children emulate the behavior of their parents, their older brothers and sisters, their friends, their teachers, and by what they see on TV. They do not, and cannot, differentiate the good from the bad. They learn it all; they absorb everything like sponges. If a child is told that they cannot do it, that they are not smart enough, that they are too small, girls do not do that, and boys are not supposed to cry, then that is what they learn. They also learn to stuff their feelings, hide their Spirit, and try to live behind the mask of acceptability, and all the while their pain shows through in their actions and words.

I think the games of "Make Believe" are the most interesting games that kids play games like: dress up, army, doctor, I Spy, and hide-and-go-seek. Many of the cartoons and kid television shows are made with this same "let's make believe" concept. These games and shows help to inspire their minds, and lets them dream of how things could be. However, at the same time, they learn, at least subconsciously, that certain people are supposed to act certain ways. If they are to be a doctor, soldier, or teacher, they must wear the appropriate mask, and live within the appropriate box. Children watch their parents' behaviors very closely, and learn the boundaries that the parents have set for their own lives. As children grow and learn, they test not only the boundaries that their parents have set for them, but also the boundaries that parents have set for themselves. This is one reason parenting can be such an emotional and trying experience.

As children grow, they begin trying on the different masks of behavior and personality that they have learned in the games they play. They try the different masks on, with their unsuspecting parents, to gain the favors they wish to obtain. Learning by trial and error, when they find a mask that works, they repeat the behavior over and over again. When they find a mask or a behavior that does not work, they suppress the behavior. If they are not allowed to express their feelings or their wonderful Spirit, they suppress it. Consequently, they learn to suppress both their gifts and their pains under a variety of different masks. They also learn that masks tend to work better with different people and in different circumstances. They unknowingly learn to put on masks that hide their true divine nature. They forget their spiritual identity and purpose, hiding the child-like innocence and natural inner beauty that we are meant to express.

Likewise, we have learned to wear the mask that helped us get what we want. One mask brings us love, success, and happiness, while another mask protects us from many of life's challenges. In certain situations, we will wear another mask that keeps others from getting too close, and still another mask that allows us to hide our pain. Unfortunately, we learn to experience life from behind these masks, and have come to believe that we are somehow separate from God. Then, we wonder why life seems so incomplete.

My wife once took me to see the movie, *What Women Want*[3] Do you think that was a hint? It was an interesting movie. It highlighted how we have learned to wear different masks to meet the needs of the world, while underneath the mask our feelings, and our fears, and our pains create turmoil within us. How rare it is, when we find a safe place to share our true inner feelings and thoughts; the result is that we experience the feelings of loneliness. What we all want is someone to listen to us, to appreciate us, and to acknowledge our feelings.

Viewing life through the illusions of the mask that we have donned, we come to realize that our life is incomplete, and we experience all sorts of inner turmoil and pain. This inner turmoil and pain is a call for us to awaken to our true natures, and to let go of those masks that we have been hiding behind. The pain we feel is supposed to be an early warning system to let us know we have gotten off the track; it is a call for healing. However, we tend to ignore these signals. These impulses of restlessness and longing are actually a deep inner desire to know Love's Presence. If we could only realize that in all our interactions with others *"there is only love, or a call for love."*[4] Either we know Love's Presence through our experiences, or we cry out for It in whatever way we have learned.

Unfortunately, the way many of us have learned to call for God's love is by inappropriate behavior. We have masked our call for God with anger and violence, and we react out of fear. When we do not deal with our pain, it causes conflict, turmoil, and disease. However, it really is not a question of whether or not we deal with our pain, but *how* we will deal with it. We can ignore these calls to awaken and continue to feel the effects in our bodies and lives, or we can seek to heal the pain that lies beneath the mask. However, we must feel our pain, in order to heal it and move through it. The healing comes in feeling the pain, expressing the pain appropriately, then forgiving and releasing it. The act of forgiving will lift our thoughts from anger or pain, to a higher awareness of Love's Presence. As we release the pain through the process of forgiveness, we finally come to realize we have hidden a part of ourselves beneath the masks we wear. We have hidden our feelings, our thoughts, and our

---

3   <u>What Women Want</u>, Paramount Pictures 2000, starring Mel Gibson & Helen Hunt

4   A Course In Miracles, The Foundation of Inner Peace, Tiburon CA

dreams; we have suppressed our Spirit. We come to realize that we have lived our life in a box, whose boundaries have been created by what we perceive others expect of us. It is time to let go of the mask, and express our authentic self.

The Oscar-winning movie "Nell," speaks to the heart of this issue. Nell speaks in her own defense in front of the judge, who is about to determine her fate. Nell says, "I was afraid. Everyone is frightened, everywhere. The good Lord sees our pain, and the Lord soothes our tears our many tears. You have big things. You know big things, but you don't look into each other's eyes, and you hunger for quietness and love. I have a small life, know small things, but I know quietness and I know loved ones."

Jesus taught us, "Do not hold the children back, for whoever does not receive the Kingdom of God like a child shall not enter." Children live fully in the moment. They do not wear the mask to hide their feelings or their bright inner radiance of God's Spirit. Their intuition is remarkably clear, and they have a natural knowledge of Spirit that can be incredible. We already have, within our essence, all the knowledge we will ever need to experience the longings of our hearts. I have heard it said that we are here on Earth, in this schoolroom, to learn to love. Learning to *love* is what life is all about. Jesus commanded us over and over again "to love one another." As long as we hold on to the mask, we will never experience the fullness of God's love. So, I invite you to let go of whatever mask you might be wearing, and allow your inner essence to express Itself in this moment now. Let go and let your Spirit express through you, and you will know God's love.

One with Spirit, I remove the mask that hides that truth of who I am,
and I experience the fullness of life!

Resources of this chapter

- A Course In Miracles, The Inner Peace Foundation, Tiburon, CA

- What You Can Feel You Can Heal, A Guide for Enriching Relationships, John Gray, Ph.D., Heart Publications, Mill Valley CA

- Nell, Twentieth Century Fox 1994

- What Women Want, Paramount Pictures 2000, Starring Mel Gibson and Helen Hunt

- The Holy Bible, New Revised Standard Version

No Evil: You've Got To Be Kidding!

"There is only One Presence and One Power in the Universe and in my life, God the Good"

A little old lady answered a knock at the door, only to be confronted by a well-dressed young man, carrying a vacuum cleaner. "Good morning," the young man said. "If I could take a couple of minutes of your time, I would like to demonstrate the very latest in high-powered vacuum cleaners."

"Go away!" said the old lady. "I haven't got any money! I'M BROKE!!!" She tried to close the door, but quick as a flash, the young man wedged his foot in the door and pushed it wide open, and said, "Don't be too hasty! Not until you have at least seen my demonstration." And, with a quick motion, he emptied a big bucket of yucky mush out onto her hallway carpet. "If this vacuum cleaner does not remove all traces of this yucky mush from your carpet, Madam, I will personally eat the remainder."

The old lady stepped back and said, "Well, I hope you've got a pretty good appetite, this morning they cut my electricity off."

So, would you say that was a good or a bad thing to do? Spiritually, we know that it was neither good nor bad, that it is just what it is. Although, most people would agree it really was not very smart.

On my last trip to Unity, in Chicago, I found my friend Frieda, sitting on the steps of the church and crying. Frieda had been physically battered for many years during her marriage. Recently she'd found the courage to move out of that abusive relationship, and develop a new life based on spiritual principles. Her new life had been a struggle between her former ingrained beliefs and her new evolving ones. With courage and faith, she had moved through many of her fears, doubts, and limiting beliefs. One of her deepest desires was that her two daughters would not experience the pain and anguish of an abusive relationship. She was painfully aware that they might have learned the self-limiting, defeating lifestyle that she demonstrated during her abusive marriage, and she often prayed to God that they would be spared such a relationship.

Now this had happened and she had lost all hope; the damage had been done. Through her tears and grasps for air, Frieda shared with me the hideous torture her eldest daughter had endured, before she was strangled to death by her live-in boy friend, leaving her daughter's two young children without any type of guardianship.

Frieda cried out "No Evil! You have got to be kidding?" Her story and her words made an impression on my heart. Frieda feared what the state would do with her two grandchildren. She wanted to raise them herself, but she feared that she might produce the same results as she did with her daughter, setting her grandchildren up for the same fate as their mother.

One of the most difficult concepts for a Truth Student to grasp is that God is absolute good, and that there is no evil. It is a concept that appears to contradict our physical reality. All you have to do is pick up a newspaper, or watch the news, and you will be confronted by the evil and sin that exists in our human experience. How can God be absolute good, if He allows such tremendous turmoil and grief to exist? There are a multitude of shades of darkness that we could describe as evil.

I do not know about you, but I was raised with the belief that there was a "force" that was in rebellion against God, because God dictates and controls our lives. Therefore, you had better watch out, or the fallen forces of God's former family would take you in, and then you would burn in the fires of hell forever. Life certainly can be a precarious experience. No evil! You have got to be kidding? But, then there are those experiences in life that lead us into a deeper experience of the *infinite*: spiritual experiences like the one Paul had on the road to Damascus was rendered blind; like the one Myrtle Fillmore had when she was told she had tuberculosis and would soon die;[5] and yes, even like the one Frieda had. Each of these experiences, which appeared to be extremely negative or evil" at first, ultimately lift those individuals to an awareness of Spirit's Presence, and to a result that could only be described as miraculous. If we are able to break through our pains and our fears long enough, we would be able to see that Spirit is working in the midst of every challenge, urging us to awaken to a greater reality. Kahlil Gibran, a Lebanese author and poet, said it best: "Pain is the breaking of the shell that encloses our understanding."[6] If somehow we could allow our awareness to be opened to the spiritual dimension of reality, we would come into a deeper understanding of Life and the Laws that regulate its ebb and flow. We would gain a very different understanding of what people have termed "evil."

I cannot say that I have ever had a 2 x 4 experience (as I call them) like that of the Apostle Paul; however, I did have a series of experiences in what might be called a gradual awakening. The greatest of these challenges was with a man named Terry B. I had had a succession of bad bosses, and I found myself moving from one job to the next, primarily to get away from my boss. Each of these bosses was mean, demanding, unreasonable, and hateful. However, every time I would leave one job and go to the next, I found that same person, only somehow they were wearing a different body and had grown meaner and more hateful. I remember thinking, "How could there be so many mean and horrible bosses? It must be the restaurant industry that attracts them." (At this time I had worked in the restaurant industry for 21 years.)

So, the next time I switched jobs, I switched industries and found the worst of the worst. Terry B. was the owner of a small courier business that made deliveries of radioactive pharmaceuticals across ten states, from a northern suburb of Chicago picking up the packages at six o'clock in the evening and delivering them by eight the next morning. It was not long before I realized why my fellow employees referred to Terry as, "Hitler's evil twin." Terry ran the business very strictly and with a firm hand on approach. If he had a question, or thought something was wrong, he went straight to the source and let them have it. You have to love that

5   Myrtle Fillmore, Mother of Unity, Unity Books, Unity Village MO

6   The Prophet, Kahlil Gibran, Alfred A. Knopf, New York, New York

approach, but Terry only knew one way to talk, which was to by yelling at the top of his lungs. If there was a mistake, he was sure to find it, and take a weird delight in pointing out his employee's shortcomings over and over again.

Terry was very punctual and his behavior very obsessive. Each morning, he would arrive at 8:00 am on the dot - not a minute early or late. You could set your watch by him. It was as if he stood outside the door, ready for the precise moment his watch would strike eight, before opening the door to the office. Two minutes later, he would walk into operations and begin screaming, at the top of his lungs, about whatever he thought might be wrong. Now, mind you, this courier business operated with a 99.9% on-time delivery rate, across a ten state area. You might think, considering the delivery range, this boss would be glowing.

Fortunately for me, I worked the midnight to noon shift (well, at least it was finally a five-day work week, something very different from the restaurant industry). I only had to manage four hours a day with him, but it was enough to set my nerves on edge. It got to the point that I was getting physically sick, just before his arrival each morning, from the stress and the fear of not knowing what would set him off.

It was about this time that I started attending Unity. I told myself, if this stuff Unity teaches really works, I would be able to use it right there. So, each morning at seven o'clock, I would stop whatever I was doing, and take time for prayer, asking Spirit to show me what I must do. How could I be an instrument of love and peace, so that this situation could be resolved? I would ask Spirit to reveal what needed to be revealed. Each morning the meditation grew deeper and I grew more peaceful. I would visualize Terry standing before me, seeing him immersed in a radiant golden light, and I would affirm, "The Christ in me greets the Christ in thee."

Then, one morning, a very strange thing happened during my prayer time. I saw a wounded child emerge from Terry's chest. When Terry arrived that morning, right at eight, I was calm and peace filled. Terry broke the silence, a few minutes later, and came into our department, yelling at the tops of his lungs about who knows what. In that moment, Spirit prompted me what to do and say. I stood up, walked over to Terry, looked him directly into his eyes, and quietly said, "You know, Terry, I have extremely good hearing, but you are speaking so loudly it is difficult for me to understand what you are saying. I you could speak more softly I would be happy to explain or do whatever you would like." Terry, who had been red in the face a few moments earlier, took a deep breath, looked at me quietly, turned around and left.

A few moments later, he came back and asked his question in an appropriate manner. For the remainder of my time working there, Terry never raised his voice again, to me, or anyone else in the office. A few weeks later, Terry declared Friday to be employee appreciation day and would buy lunch for all the staff. During this time, he began to share portions of his childhood with us. He grew up in a very poor part of West Virginia, and was raised by a physically abusive and domineering mother. He rarely had enough to eat. His father was an alcoholic, who left home when Terry was two. He had very few friends, and although he was in his forties, he had never gone out on a date. His work was his life. Yelling, being demanding, and acting tough was the way he learned to communicate. Terry had been calling out for love in the only way he knew.

This was a huge learning experience for me. Things are not always as they appear to be; and people who might be considered bad or evil, really are not bad or evil. Something horrible had gone wrong, somewhere in their life, and they are just trying to cover their hurt and pain - just trying to survive. Often things that harm others are done with the best of intentions, either through misguided vision, or from the frustration of the perpetrator's hopes and dreams. People call out for love and support in the only way they know how.

After this incident, my own suppressed memories and fears began to come out of the darkness of my subconscious mind. I remembered how my parents would have violent and explosive arguments, night after night after night. My brothers, sisters, and I learned first hand not to get involved, or in the middle, or we would suffer the consequences. So we all found our own hiding places. My hideout was under the china cabinet. It was a huge china cabinet, which I could disappear under and find safety. Consequently, as a young adult, whenever I was confronted by an angry, demanding, violent person, I would normally disappear (at least mentally and emotionally) and go to my hideout. Or, as would happen on occasion, I would explode with the anger I was suppressing, which only frightened me more. When I was confronted by demanding, forceful bosses who were repressing their angers and resentments, I was shown a reflection of myself, a part of me I did not like, and it made me very uncomfortable. So I fled, but wherever I went ... there I was! Each time I fled, my "healing need" would only call out louder. Spirit kept calling for me to awaken.

The Star Wars movie, *The Empire Strikes Back*, highlighted this concept for me. Luke Skywalker, the now famous Jedi Knight, was about to enter a cave. Luke looks at Yoda, the Jedi master, and says, "Something is not right here; I feel cold, death."

Yoda responds, "That place is strong with the dark side, and as long as it remains, evil it is. But you must go there."

Luke asks, "What is in there?"

Yoda replied, "Only what you take with you."

Luke enters, and is exploring the cave when his archenemy, Darth Vader, appears. A fight ensues. When Luke finally triumphs, he finds that the face behind the mask of the person he was fighting was his own.[7]

What we fear most is the darkness we have hidden deep within ourselves. We then project this darkness out into the world around us. The darkness is the reflection of our fears, our angers, and our own perception. Literally, it is what we have brought with us.

Often, the erratic behavior and anger we see in others is the result of the way they have learned to survive, in what they believe is a chaotic, hostile world. We have drawn these individuals into our lives because, at some level of our being, they resonate with our own healing needs. Likewise, they are called to us for the opportunity to heal their issues. Just as Spirit had brought Terry and me together so that we could each heal the woundedness that was lying, unhealed, deep within. We can recognize these forces of growth and change, but to heal them we have to surrender to them by looking for a deeper understanding of our feelings and emotions. The other option is to resist this healing dynamic and label it evil, but then we are doomed to repeat this pattern over and over again. However, the truth is we are struggling with forces that seek to bring healing and harmony to our souls.

---

7   *The Empire Strikes Back*, George Lucas and Lucas Films

Things are not often as they would appear to be, and we need to look deeper. The Universe is a living, growing, changing reality and at the core of this reality is the *Infinite Oneness*. It is the *life-force* flowing within you. God is all there is. Just as the laws of science guide the working of the planets, the stars, and the cycles of life, here on our planet there are certain laws of being that guide the evolution of the Spirit we were created to be. Nothing can work in opposition to it and go unaffected, and nothing can work outside it.

When we break the Laws of Being, we suffer the consequence, even if we are not aware that the "Law" exists. When we fall short of the mark of our highest potential, whatever we have set into motion must be atoned for, not as a punishment, but rather to heal and resolve the negative vibration we have set forth or repressed. God does not punish us for what we have done, but the law is the law. Consequently, we reap the results of what we have sown. It is the harvest of our own negative thoughts and actions. Unfortunately, instead of searching for the underlying cause of what we have sown, and changing the life pattern that has caused it, we have learned to call these negative manifestations "evil," and project it onto the people and the world around us.

But you know God warned us! Yes, God warned us about the human tendency to judge and to be polarized by the appearances of duality. It is recorded in the book of Genesis that, way back at the beginning of time, Jehovah took Adam aside and showed him around the garden, and gave him the power to name and label everything he saw. Then Jehovah cautioned Adam, "You may freely eat of every tree of the garden; but of *the Tree of the Knowledge of Good and Evil* you shall not eat, for in the day that you eat of it you shall die." I think that is a pretty clear-cut warning.

Well, we all know what happened a little later. Eve was persuaded by that annoying little snake, and partook of the fruit of the Tree of the Knowledge of Good and Evil. Adam followed suit. However, did they die? No, many other things did happen but they did not die a physical death. If Adam and Eve had died, how could they be considered the ancestors of all mankind? In fact, they lived a long and full life. So, was God just bluffing and making big idle threats as many parents do today? No, the fact is that they did experience a type of death; they died to God's awareness. They believed themselves to be separate from God and the Oneness of the garden.

The words "sleep," "die," and "dead" were often used metaphorically in the Bible to imply living outside the awareness of God, indicating that we are unconscious of the divine. To "die" is to lack the realization of God's presence, believing we are outside God's "garden of Life." Adam and Eve did not die in a physical way when they ate the fruit, nor could they in truth, for they were created in the image and likeness of God (Genesis 1:27). Jesus said, "God is Spirit" – "God is the Breath of Life," meaning God is the very essence of life itself. The truth is our Spirit - the light within this clay bodysuit - cannot die. However, while in these garments of flesh we can fall into the darkness of believing that we are somehow separate from the Oneness of the Spectrum of Life and Light, and become subject to the battle that is brought forth from eating of the fruits of the knowledge of good and evil. This was the death that Jehovah had warned Adam about, when he told him not to eat of the fruit of the Tree of Knowledge of Good and Evil.

Likewise, when we bite into that tasty - looking piece of fruit, we enter into a realm of the mortal mind caught between perceived good and evil.

The mortal mind lives in a world of dualities, constantly being asked to choose between opposites—night or day, good or bad, love or hate, past or future, action or reaction. When we become caught in a constant motion of the mind, we are unable to experience the stillness of the now moment, where wholeness and oneness in the Infinite resides. That place of stillness is right there in the midst of us.

When we believe in the duality that results from eating of the fruits of the Tree of Knowledge of Good and Evil, we judge others. We believe that there can be something other than the oneness of Spirit's Presence, and we experience the darkness of separation. Many people walk in the darkness. Jesus referred to them as the walking dead, and told us, "Let your light shine into the darkness."

The tragedy of Eden is that it is being re-enacted every day. Each time we make a judgment as to whether something is good or bad, right or wrong, we bite into the fruit of the Tree of the Knowledge of Good and Evil, and die to the awareness of the Kingdom, giving power to the illusions of evil and darkness. Do you remember Jesus' warning? "Judge not, for with what judgment you judge, you shall be judged and the measure you mete, it shall be measured unto you." (Matthew 7:1 –2) This statement is a basic law of the universe: as you give, so shall you receive. Whatever thought you send out will come back to you. Later he added, "Judge not by appearance, but judge with right thinking."

Why do you think a loving God would put that tree in the middle of the garden, if he did not want Adam and Eve to eat from it? The Infinite One could have simply removed the tree. I have never understood how a loving Father, that Jesus taught about, could punish generation after generation of humankind for an error committed by the first of their kind. That does not seem to be very loving at all, nor is it very logical. And do you not think that an all-knowing, all-powerful, infinitely wise Creator of the universe probably should have known that, if He placed a really good-looking piece of candy in front of a child, that more than likely the child would eat it—even if he was told not to? How many mothers know that? So, I think that "One" who is *all knowing* probably would know that if He really wanted to keep a child (or, for that matter, anyone) from eating something that looks really good, he should keep it out of sight. If it was something really important, like the fruit of the Tree of the Knowledge of Good and Evil, it just might need to be locked up!

I believe Jehovah warned Adam not to eat that tempting fruit, just like any good parent would warn their child not to become involved in something that could harm them. How many parents have tried to warn their children about being burned by a stove, and still the child manages to burn itself. You cannot take the stove out of the house; it is an essential part of any home. Eventually the child will learn how to use it, just as we each will eventually learn to use our faculties of discernment in the proper way.

The Be-Attitude, "Blessed are the pure in heart, for they shall see God," (Matt 5:8) gives us an insight to our struggle with good and evil. When we are pure in heart, we are established in our spiritual essence; we see all things through the single eye of Spirit. We see only the goodness that God created. Duality does not exist; that is we do not see good or evil in any situation—only what is. We see other people with compassion and understanding, including those who sometimes find themselves in desperate situations and call out for love and understanding in the only way they know how. When we live from this point of view, we live with power and experience our wholeness. However, most of us have learned to view life with our five senses; therefore, we perceive a world full of limitations and human manifestations. We form the belief that we are separate from God, and separate from the good we seek. This belief in separation is where our duality begins; it is the root of all that can be described as evil in God's creation of good.

When we learn to view life from our spiritual essence, we see beyond appearance to the innate potential of all. At times, it is really hard to see the good in all situations, especially like the one Frieda experienced; however, it is there—we simply have to look deeper. Frieda later told me that good did come out of her experience that the experience had been a turning point in her life. She gained custody of her two grandchildren. Feeling she had been offered a new opportunity at life, she seized the opportunity and greeted it with enthusiasm and joy, which attracted more joy into her life.

How will we know the light from the darkness in our life? The ways of Spirit will never cause us to seek control, power, or influence, or cause us to seek retribution or hide. It will not leave us thinking, "No Evil! You have got to be kidding!" Spirit will always guide us in the ways of love, be experienced with joy, and result in peace. When we are calm, at peace, and passive, we will know the stirring of Spirit deep within our souls. It will lift our hearts and inspire our minds. We will know that God is all there is, and that there is nothing to fear.

"There is only One Presence and One Power in the Universe and in my life, God the Good"

Resources for this Chapter

- The Prophet, Kahlil Gibran, Alfred A. Knopf, New York, NY

- Myrtle Fillmore, Mother of Unity, Unity Books, Unity Village MO

- The Empire Strikes Back, George Lucas and Lucas Films

- Dynamics for Living Charles Fillmore, Unity Books, Unity Village, MO

- Lesson In Truth, Emilie Cady, Unity Books, Unity Village MO

- What You Feel You Can Heal, Dr. John Gray, Heart Publishing, Mill Valley, CA

- The Eye of the Storm, Gary Simmons, Unity Books, Unity Village MO

- Radical Forgiveness, Colin Tippin, Global 13 Publications, Inc Marietta, GA

- The Holy Bible, New Revised Standard Version

Clinging to the Rocks

I surrender to the flow of life and allow the Sacred Spirit to lift me to new heights.

— 66 —

"Once upon a time there lived a village of creatures along the bottom of a great crystal river. Each creature, in its own manner, clung tightly to the twigs and rocks of the river bottom, for clinging was their way of life, and resisting the current is what each had learned from birth.

"But one creature said at last, 'I am tired of clinging. Though I cannot see it with my eyes, I trust that the current knows where it is going. I shall let go and let the river take me where it will. For in clinging I shall surely die of boredom.' Taking a breath, he let go. The current lifted him free from the bottom, and he was bruised and hurt no more.

"Now the creatures downstream, to whom he was a stranger, cried, 'See a miracle! A creature like ourselves, yet he flies! See the Messiah, come to save us all!'

"The one carried in the current said, 'I am no more a Messiah than you. The river delights to lift us free, if only we dare let go. Let go and you to shall fly free. Our true work is this voyage, this adventure."

"But they cried 'Savior!' all the while clinging to the rocks, and when they looked again he was gone, and they were left alone making legends of a Savior." [8]

99

This is the prologue of Richard Bach's book, *Illusions*—an insightful and powerful allegory about the way many people cling to their illusions of reality, all the while allowing the stream of life to flow over them, resisting the currents because it is the way of life they had been taught. For centuries our civilization has chosen to make saviors, even deities, out of those we revere—not only religious figures like Jesus and Buddha but also athletes, musicians, and actors. We focus on their goodness and their insights and their successes, all the while clinging to the rocks of our own personal fears and limiting beliefs that restrict their lives. Our culture has built a vast system of beliefs on what appears to be stable knowledge of the physical world, but this knowledge has not always proven to be reliable. When one of these rocks of knowledge suddenly is dis-proven, our world falls into chaos, and people fight back, clinging to what they have known despite the evidence of current findings.

In Jesus' time, they believed the world to be both flat and the center of the universe; we were God's special creation all alone in the universe. When Columbus had a theory that he could sail west and reach India, he had to flee from Italy where they thought he was insane. Eventually, Columbus was able to convince the Spanish to give him three small ships for his unlikely venture. When Galileo made the first telescope and theorized that the earth and the other planets revolved around the sun and not the earth, he was tried for heresy. There are countless examples of this tendency to cling to the rocks of our knowing. It has not been easy for humankind to give up some of its cherished beliefs—even long after they have been proved not to be true. We cling to them and try to make them work, but they do not. Just as some people cling to the theory of creationism today. While others cannot fathom that our bodies are not solid parts, but rather a collection of cells composed mostly of energy, as physics and quantum physics are proving today.

---

8   *Illusions, The Adventures of a Reluctant Messiah*, Richard Bach, Dell Publishing Co, New York, New York

All the world is changing rapidly: our beliefs, how we live, travel, and treat one another. Having a child in your life only brings that point home all the more quickly. Every few months I look at my daughter and say, "How did you get so big?" She is not the same precious little child of two and three anymore; she is so much more.

We teach our children their core beliefs through our words and actions. They will live with those beliefs as their foundation, as their rock, and will perceive the world through what we have taught them—just as our parents, and the world around us, have taught *us*. What if some of those beliefs and perceptions are wrong, or out of focus? Will we cling to them? Will we continue to cling to the rocks and twigs at the bottom of the river of life, resisting the current simply because it is the way we were taught?

Spirit continually beckons to us from deep within: "Trust that the current knows where it is going, and that the river of life delights to lifts you free—if only you dare to let go and let God." Our true work is in the adventure, in the experience, and that work is learning and understanding our true identity as spiritual beings.

In his own way, Jesus often referred to the human tendency to cling to rocks. Or I should say, he spoke about the human tendency to cling to our daily lives and to worry and be anxious about life. In Jesus' time, people spent much of their thought and energy focused in worry and anxiety about how they were going to get by from day-to-day and week-to-week—in terms of food, clothing, and housing. Have you ever found yourself worrying about how you were going to make it, concerned about how to pay the bills? How about the price of gasoline? "What if there is an accident? How will I get by?" Here is what Jesus had this to say about such habits:

66

"Therefore I tell you, do not worry about your life, what you will eat or what you will drink, or about your body, what you will wear; is not life more than food, and the body more than clothing? Look at the birds of the air; they neither sow nor reap nor gather into barns, and yet your heavenly Father feeds them. Are you not of more value than they? Can any of you by worrying add a single hour to your span of life? Why do you worry about clothing? Consider the lilies of the field, how they grow, they neither toil nor spin, yet I tell you even Solomon in all his glory was not clothed like one of these ... Will he not much more clothe you? You of little faith! Therefore do not worry, saying 'What will we eat?' or 'What will we drink?' or 'What will we wear?' Your heavenly Father knows that you need all these things. But strive first for the Kingdom and Its harmony[9], and all these things will be given to you as well." (Matthew 6:25 New Revised Standard Version and Aramaic translation.)

99

The first time I heard this teaching from the Sermon on the Mount, I was filled with a complete sense of peace, of well-being, of value. It was overwhelming; I was probably thirty-five or thirty-six at the time. I thought, "Me! I am of *great value*! And my Father? *My Father in Heaven* will provide for me as well as he does for the birds and the lilies of the field, and the rest of nature!" According to the Bible, you and I were created in the image and likeness of our Heavenly Father, the creative force of the universe; whose image and likeness, if we are to believe Jesus, "is Spirit and life!" (John 4:4) We are beings of Spirit and life, innately of the *One Presence*—a Presence that flows through our being. If we first seek this Presence, we shall have all our needs met.

However, often in life we do everything *but* seek the Kingdom and Its harmony. We become so focused on the challenges and turmoil of our fast-paced lives that we fall into "the trap." In the trap, we forget; we forget our true essence as spiritual beings, and we begin to believe that our physical appearance is our true identity. We give our possessions, our jobs, our houses—*our rocks*—a place of highest importance in our life. These symbols of God's love become our complete reality. We believe they represent who we are, and what we have achieved. Then we become anxious and start to worry about how we are going to maintain it all. We separate ourselves in consciousness from God and believe we have acquired our abundance all on our own. "The belief in separation from

---

9   *The Prayers of the Cosmos,* Neil Douglas-Koltz, Harper & Row Publishers, San Francisco - Translation of the Aramaic Texts of New Testaments

God is the root of all human suffering."[10] Emily Cady wrote these words, way back *1903*, but we still have not figured it out.

Anxieties and worries, about material necessities of life, divert our attention away from seeking the Kingdom and Its harmony. Anxiety and worry are quite natural emotions, and there are certainly times when they serve a purpose; however, when these emotions become an attitude or way of being, their negativity is reflected in every area of our body and our affairs. In times of concern, we begin to cling to our possessions and our physical identity. The more tightly we hold on, the more tension and stress develops within us. Joy and pleasure disappear. Life becomes a dreary, dismal, stressful experience. In a very real sense, an attitude of anxiety and worry is a rejection of God and God's Kingdom of abundance, because we believe that we are separate from God, and live outside of Its domain of grace and abundance. Indeed, *"The belief that we are somehow separate from God is the root of all human suffering."*

As a result of the way we live, we have created walls in our minds by clinging to beliefs that limit us, and prevent us from seeing beyond the appearance of our circumstances. We cling to various limiting beliefs, restricting perception, and outright illusion, despite how illogical they might be or how much pain they create. Part of our problem is something pointed out by the movie *What the Bleep Do We Know, which shares* "We cannot see, or recognize, a different pattern or possibility until we acknowledge, and become open to the fact, that other possibilities might exist."[11] This keeps us stuck, clinging to the same beliefs until something drastic happens—a "2 x 4 experience"—and even then, we are lucky if we realize that an alternative might be available. Hopefully, the event causes us to rethink our choices.

Kahlil Gibran, a Middle Eastern philosopher and poet, shared these words of wisdom about such experiences: "Pain is the breaking of the shell that encloses our understanding."[12] So often, it is the pain we experience that finally causes us to push through the wall of fear, anxiety, stress,

---

10 *Lesson In Truth,* Emilie Cady, Unity Books, Unity Village Missouri

11 *What the Bleep Do We Know?* Twentieth Century Fox Entertainment

12 The Prophet, Kahlil Gibran, Alfred A. Knopf publisher, New York, New York

and anger we have enclosed ourselves within. Pain is often our true self, our spiritual essence, trying to burst through the boundaries we have created in our thinking, seeking to push us to move through the darkness to grasp an understanding of the Truth of who we are, a seed of potential made in the image and likeness of God.

For many years, I pursued life in this manner, looking to outer appearances for satisfaction. All the while, I felt an inner restlessness that was never quite satisfied. I searched and searched—in athletics, alcohol, drugs, and work—but I could not fill the emptiness. Even when my life was seemingly going well, I knew that something was missing, and I felt that happiness and success were outside my reach. I was placing my self-worth, self-esteem, and happiness in outer appearances. I clung tightly to all that I felt was part of my world, even though I knew it was lacking. Tension filled my life; it was certainly dreary, dismal, and stressful. However, I was afraid, if I let go of what I was holding onto so tightly, what would I Have? What would I be? Would I not become lost? However, there came a time when I found I was so immersed in the darkness of despair, I felt like my life was crumbling; it seemed there was no escape from the ruins that surely lay ahead. However, deep within me the seed of my spiritual potential was stretching forth its roots, calling for nurturing, and created a desire within me to experience more of life. This was about the same time my wife found herself in a state of personal crisis. Of course, I was drawn into the pain of the crisis along with her. Neither one of us was very happy. Our life was in turmoil, and we were not having any fun at all. My wife was in so much pain, she cried out, "God help me!" It was God who guided her to the answers. One of the answers was finding Unity Church in Chicago, where she started attending regularly.

At first, I would not have anything to do with this new habit. I had enough of organized religions while I was growing up. I believed in God, but not in religions. Where I found God was in the forest of the Blue Ridge Mountains of Virginia, where I attended high school and college. I could more easily feel God's presence there, simply walking in the peace and beauty of nature. However, my wife was soon attending church three, four, and sometimes five days a week. I began to wonder what she was really doing, especially since this church was forty miles from our home.

As time went on, I noticed my wife's whole manner of being started to change. She went from being very depressed and crying all the time, to being happy with a radiant glow.

Then I really wondered what she was doing! So, I started to ask her questions about the philosophy of the church she was attending. Surprisingly, the answers were very close to my own personal philosophy, which I had developed through my own studies and observations—something we had never talked about. Church talk had been off limits. One day I decided I would attend church with her. Was she ever shocked! As I entered the church, I felt as if I had come home. I had never realized that there were other people who held similar beliefs about God. The service was upbeat, had plenty of good music, and I left feeling inspired. It was very different than any church service I had ever attended. I was hooked.

Sometime later, I was really able to hear and understand Jesus' statement in the Gospel of Mark 1:15: "The time is fulfilled, the Kingdom of God is at hand, repent and believe in the gospel." Two key words brought about this realization. The first was "repent," which was translated from a word that meant to turn or to change direction.[13] The other word was "Gospel," which really means good news. So, for me this verse is more accurately translated, "The time is now, the Kingdom of God is within your grasp, change your mind—turn to it—and believe in the good news." (Mark 1:15 NRSV) I realized the good news Jesus was trying to share with us is that "the Kingdom of God" is here now, in this moment. It is all about us. It is within us; we simply need to shift our awareness and awaken to that inner Light and Life.

This realization marked the beginning of my process of spiritual awakening. The more I have studied, prayed, and worked on forgiveness issues, and the more I listened to that quiet Inner Voice, the more I was able to catch glimpses and experiences of our Father's Kingdom, which is all around us. I realized that what I had been searching for most of my life was already within me, in my own personal relationship with the Infinite One. All I need do was to let go of what I had been clinging to, and trust Spirit to guide me.

---

13 <u>The Revealing Word</u>, Charles Fillmore, Unity Books, Unity Village MO

I remember the first time I really trusted Spirit to guide me. My wife, Yvonne, and I decided to go to a hot-air balloon festival in St. Charles, Illinois—a beautiful and quaint old town that sits along the Fox River, about an hour from where we lived. As we approached St. Charles, I asked Yvonne for the directions to the site where the balloon festival was being held. She did not know; she thought I knew where I was going. I guess that was our first mistake! So we did the unthinkable, at least from my perspective, we stopped and asked for directions (*you know how guys are about asking for directions.)* Unfortunately, no one seemed to know where this balloon festival was being held. We found ourselves faced with a couple of choices: going home, doing something else, or simply trusting Spirit to guide us.

So, we decided to take a moment to pray and let Spirit guide us. We took a big breath and allowed ourselves to be very still and just listen. We did not get any grand revelation, but each of us felt we would be able to find the festival. After the short prayer, we were on our way. Something deep within me told me to turn left off the main highway and drive down along the river for a while. Then, without any reason, I made a right turn. Yvonne cried out, "Where are you going?"

I replied, "Something told me we're supposed to turn here." I drove a few blocks, turned down an apparent dead end, and stopped. Sitting there, I laid my head down on the steering wheel and asked out loud, "Okay God, where are the balloons?" Suddenly, a very strange, long, repetitive hissing sound surrounded us. It came again and again, and then slowly, magnificently, a big, beautiful hot-air balloon arose over the trees at the end of the street. God is so awesome!

It has also been awesome watching my daughter Shavonne play as she has grown up. It reinforces my belief in God and in the activity of Spirit, which is always flowing through us. One day, when she was four, Shavonne began searching our house with her Barney flashlight. I asked her what she was looking for and, as she disappeared down the hallway, she responded, "God … but I can't find him anywhere." A few minutes later, she returned and said, "I found him. He was in my closet." God is always there, waiting for us in the inner chambers of our heart and mind.

Now, no one expects four year olds to prepare their own dinners, or infants to change their own diapers, children rely on their parents to provide for their needs. They naturally trust so completely, and in doing so, they radiate God's presence. They live in the moment, and experience life as a constant adventure, with deep curiosity and innocence. They do not worry or become anxious about what they are going to eat or wear tomorrow. It is so easy to see the activity of Spirit, and the nature of God, in children. They have not yet learned to cling to the bottom of the river of life.

Jesus, seeing this same dynamic, said that in order for us to enter the Kingdom of Heaven we must become as little children. Jesus had that childlike innocence, and held a great trust that he would be provided for, that our Father would work through him, and through each of us. Remember, the Christ within you already knows how to be a child of Spirit, and of faith, and to allow the Father within to do the work for you. Allow the awareness of that natural childlike innocence and trust to rise up into your consciousness. We do not need to struggle and cling to rocks at the bottom of river of life.

The one carried in the current said, "*I am no more a Messiah than you. The river delights to lift us free, if only we dare let go and let God, and you shall fly free. Our true work is this voyage, this adventure called life.*" Surrender to the flow of life and allow the current to take you to new heights. Seek the Infinite One first, by turning within in prayer, taking a breath and letting go. Stop clinging to the rocks and trust in Spirit.

I surrender to the flow of life and allow the Sacred Spirit to lift me to new heights.

Resources for this talk

- <u>Illusions, The Adventures of a Reluctant Messiah</u>, Richard Bach, Dell Publishing Co, New York, New York

- <u>Lesson In Truth</u>, Emilie Cady, Unity Books, Unity Village, Missouri.

- <u>The Prophet</u>, Kahlil Gibran, Alfred A. Knopf publisher, New York, New York

- <u>The Prayers of the Cosmos</u>, Neil Douglas-Koltz, Harper & Row Publishers, San Francisco - Translation of the Aramaic Texts of New Testaments

- <u>The Revealing Word</u>, Charles Fillmore, Unity Books, Unity Village, Missouri

- <u>What the Bleep Do We Know?</u> Twentieth Century Fox Entertainment

- <u>The Holy Bible, New Revised Standard version.</u>

Lessons in Manifestation

I am a magnet of God's good, and draw the goodness of the universe to me!

A man walked into a restaurant with a full-grown ostrich walking beside him. The waitress noticed them and went over to take their orders. The man requested, a hamburger, fries, and a Coke. Then the waitress turned to the ostrich. "What's your order?" It responded, "I'll have the same." A short time later, the waitress returned with the order. "That will be $9.40 please." The man reached into his pocket and pulled out the exact change for payment.

The next day, the man and the ostrich come again and the man said, "I'll have a hamburger, fries, and a Coke." The ostrich said, "I'll have the same." Again, the man reached into his pocket and pulled out the exact change. This became routine.

Then one day, when they walked in through the door, and the waitress asked, "The usual?" "No," said the man, "This is Friday night, so I will have a steak, a baked potato, and a salad." Of course, the ostrich said, "I'll have the same." Shortly afterward, the waitress brought the order and said, "That will be $32.62." Once again, the man pulled the exact change out of his pocket and placed it on the table. The waitress could not hold back her curiosity any longer. "Excuse me, sir. How do you manage to always come up with the exact amount every time you reach into your pocket?"

"Well," says the man, "several years ago I was cleaning the attic and found an old lamp. When I rubbed it, a Genie appeared and offered me two wishes. My first wish was that if I ever had to pay for anything, I would just put my hand in my pocket and the right amount of money would always be there." "That's brilliant!" the waitress said. "Most people would wish for a million dollars or something, but you'll always be as rich as you want for as long as you live!" "That's right," the man responded. "Whether it's a gallon of milk or a Rolls Royce, the exact money is always there."

The waitress then asked, "But, sir, what's with the ostrich?" The man sighed, paused, and then answered, "My second wish was for a tall chick with long legs, who would agree with everything I say."

This man had a really good lesson in manifestation. Be careful of what you ask for, because you might just get it. We all have such a "genie's lamp" hidden away in the corners of our mind. From time to time, we discover its hidden powers, but because we have not become accustomed to its use, we fail to direct its energy to its fullest potential and create things that we have not quite intended.

Then, sometimes in life, there will be a person, place, thing, or circumstance that will serve as a real touchstone for our learning, which will demonstrate just how to use this unrealized gift that lies deep within each and every one of us. My home on West Hutchinson Street in Chicago, Illinois was one of those places where I was able to clearly see to the heart of my challenges and transform them. While living there, I had a series of lessons in manifestation, which helped me to understand perhaps one of the greatest secrets to living fully and completely, while drawing the goodness of the universe to me. I learned that, through properly directing the power of my thoughts, I could be a magnet of God's good.

A few years after Yvonne and I began our journey in Unity some twenty years ago, we went to a prosperity workshop led by Edwene Gaines. Yvonne was inspired; she got a vision of life that she never knew existed. There was so much she wanted to do and have, and had never before felt like she could obtain or achieve it. She wanted to run her own business, have a new car, and she wanted to buy a house. At this time, we were living in a relatively small two-bedroom condo in the far northwest suburbs of Chicago. It was a little cramped and about thirty-five miles from just about everything we were doing and wanted to do. I was working downtown and Yvonne was working along the north shore of Lake Michigan in Evanston. Our condo, although affordable, was really inconvenient.

So Yvonne decided we were going to buy a house. Utilizing all the principles she had just learned at this prosperity workshop, Yvonne wrote down everything she wanted in a house: three or more bedrooms, two baths, a living room, a dining room, a full eat-in kitchen, a porch, a full basement, a nice yard, a two-car garage, close to shopping, and with easy excess to the freeway and public transportation. This is actually the short version of the long list she made. At the end of her prayer request, she wrote, "This or something better. Thank you, God." She held the list in her hands, stilled her mind, saw the light and energy of the universe flowing through it and then said a heart-felt prayer. Afterward, she folded up her prayer request and placed it in her newly purchased prayer box. I might also note she began setting aside a large portion of her check for the down payment.

Now, I thought all this was a pretty tall order, especially since we lived in Chicago and homes were pretty expensive. I had my doubts and believed the only kind of house we could afford would be a handyman special, where everything would need to be fixed.

Regardless of my beliefs and my protests, Yvonne and I began our search. Every Sunday afternoon for months, we went to open houses or toured homes with a real estate agent. Finally, exhausted, we decided to take a break and wait for the spring market. However, Yvonne held tight to her faith, focusing on her perfect idea of our new home, while I silently affirmed my own belief.

A few weeks later, Yvonne's mom visited us from out of state, letting us know, she knew the perfect real estate agent, who could help us to find the right home. "Yeah, right," we both thought. Both Yvonne and I said, "No we're worn out from looking." However, Yvonne's mom can be quite persistent, so we reluctantly agreed to look at just three more houses. As we walked up the porch of the first house, I wondered how we would finance a house, even if we found one we liked. However, as we walked through the door we both instantly knew that this was the house. The living room had a single long wall with no windows, where our 16-foot book shelving system would fit; something that few homes in the Chicago area have. This was a prerequisite for any house we would purchase. This house also had everything else on Yvonne's list: four bedrooms and a master bedroom suite, two baths, a living room, dining room, an eat-in kitchen, two porches, a full basement, two car garage, nice yard, close to shopping and easy excess to the freeway. At the same time, it had everything I had asked for—everything in the house needed to be fixed up.

One of the best-kept secrets of the ages is something called *the Law of Mind Action*, which states, "Thoughts held in mind produce after their own kind; we create our reality through the thoughts we most persistently hold in mind." The creative force of the mind is continually creating, and like fertile soil, it does not differentiate between the seed of a weed and that of a flower. It simply responds to the thoughts we most persistently hold in mind, drawing, shaping, and forming the substance of the invisible realm and bringing it into the manifest realm. Your ideas and thoughts determine what is to be created; like attracts like. The only question that remains is what type of seeds have you been planting in the fertile soil of your mind, "the seeds of weeds or the seeds of flowers?" Focus on what you want, not on the challenge or the obstacle, or the things you do not want. Make your request and then look for Spirit's response, as you prepare yourself to receive the manifesting good that is coming forth. You are a magnet of God's good. Go ahead and affirm it with me! "I am a magnet of God's good, and I draw the goodness of the universe to me!"

The first time I try explaining this concept to someone, I often hear, "I don't have that kind of power; if I did my life wouldn't be such a mess. Why would I ever consciously create something like this?" I have to agree, no one would ever consciously create the turmoil, conflict or drama that occurs in their life; we do it unconsciously as a result of the doubts, limitations, and negativity that rise up out of our core beliefs, or in response to the limiting perspective we hold about the world and the people around us. In other words, we react to the illusions of the world we see and experience. Just as, I drew into my life a house that needed many repairs; it was a true lesson in manifestation. Therefore, I began to watch what I was calling into my life through my thoughts and words and ingrained beliefs.

Most humans go through life sleepwalking, unaware of their core beliefs and how they tint their thoughts, words, and desires, consequently directing the creative power of their minds in what most of us would call a negative way. I must admit I was once the same way. When I first learned the secret of the Law of Mind Action I would stop and look at my thoughts. There was always this constant monkey chatter going on, in kind of a whirlwind of activity. My mind would leap from one thought to another to another. It was like having a little boy in my mind who had A.D.D. My mind would never stay still or become focused on one thing for any length of time. Then I looked at my life. I saw a corresponding energy. I was relatively intelligent (at least my college degree seemed to indicate that), I was hard working, motivated, insightful, got along well with others (well, most of the time, anyway), but every time I achieved some degree of success I found a way to short-circuit it, and I had no idea why. But now I do. It was the result of thoughts I persistently held in mind! I was a magnet to all that I drew into my life.

Interestingly enough, the day after we signed the agreement to purchase the house, we received the news that Yvonne would be receiving a small inheritance, enough to pay the down payment and closing costs for our new house. It is just the way Spirit works, in bringing forth things from the realm of invisible into our reality. Yvonne certainly had nothing blocking her creative potential and now the money that Yvonne had been setting aside could be used to pay for all those repairs that I had manifested. Do you think I got the message?

I can still remember the day we walked into our new home after the closing. Yvonne broke down crying! "Good God, what have we done now"? Were the only words she could utter! The sight of the house, without the furniture in it, was abysmal. In all my years of doing light home repairs, I had never seen any thing like it. The places where the furniture had been sitting had hidden the wear of the carpet and the places where the wallpaper had been holding back the sagging plaster and lath, which were beginning to collapse. The house was, after all, eighty-five years old and had been poorly maintained. It was now showing its age. Now I was the one who was holding on tightly to the vision of the house in its most perfect state.

Fortunately, we had already ordered new carpet and I had asked a few people at the church to come help paint. A group of seven people, who had just finished a yearlong project of remodeling a forty-thousand square foot replica of the Wimbledon Tennis Club, which had been built in 1924 and was going to serve as our church home, showed up to help. As people began to show up Yvonne started crying all over again. I silently held to the thought that someone would know what to do with those sagging walls; and they did. They all stayed late into the night for two evenings, painting and working on all the things that needed to be fixed before the carpet could be installed and the furniture delivered.

The vision of a beautiful home became a reality. When we walked into our new house a few days later, we were greeted by rich, plush carpeting and beautifully painted walls that were accented with crown moldings along the ceiling, and a floor reminiscent of a home built in the early nineteen hundreds. It was indeed a remarkable transformation.

When we got all the furniture into the house, we realized that although we now had a dining room, we did not have any dining room furniture. It was just an empty room. We had moved from a 1200 square foot condo into a 3,000 square foot house, and we did not have nearly enough furniture to fill it. We also did not really have any money to purchase new furniture. That would be going on the long list of things that our new home needed. Yvonne and I wrote down, on a piece a paper, that the right and perfect dining room set would manifest at just the right price, held the prayer request in our hands, saw the energy and light of the universe flowing through it, and said, "Thank You, God." We then dropped the note into the prayer box, releasing this new challenge into God's hands.

Would you believe a week later Yvonne's mom, who had just moved back to Chicago area, and not knowing we needed a dining room set, called and asked if we knew anybody who needed a nearly new dinning room set. She was working with a lady who had just purchased a new ornate set and wanted to find a place for the more modest one she had bought the year before. The lady just needed someone to come pick it up and did not want any money. We said we would be right out. It was another lesson in manifestation. "I am a magnet of God's good, and I draw the goodness of the universe to me."

We were to discover that one of the biggest problems with our new house was the kitchen. It was not the state-of-the-art kitchen I would have liked. The first problem was that it had six doors. That's right, six doors; one opened into the living room, one to the back porch, one to the upstairs, one to a large pantry, and two opened into small unusable closets. Don't ask me how we did not notice this when we were buying the house. Since the kitchen had so many doors, it had very little wall space for cabinets; there were just two small cabinets over the sink. That was it! Another unique feature of the kitchen was that if the refrigerator was running and you turned on another appliance, like the microwave or toaster oven, you blew a fuse. I am not really sure how anyone ever managed to live in the house for long, because we were continually running up and down the stairs to replace fuses. Luckily, we had already planned to do some kitchen renovations.

After a lot of thought and prayer, about what to do with the kitchen, Yvonne and I developed a plan. We created a vision in our mind of the perfect kitchen and went to work bringing the ideal and the reality together. We would close off two of the doors and have new cabinets installed in an L-shape, replacing the 1940's stove with a down-draft grill—in an island unit with a breakfast bar. With all the new updates we were planning, we would need to have some electric work done. I thought to myself, *"This is going to be big bucks, how are we going to afford all of this?"* Instantly, I caught myself in that thought, and I said "Cancel, cancel, cancel. If this vision of our perfect kitchen is meant to be, God will show us the way." Yvonne and I wrote out our vision, and attached a picture of a similar kitchen adding the note, "This or something better Lord; just show us the way." We held the prayer request in our hands, saw the light and the energy of the universe flowing through it, and said, "Thank You, God, for guiding us in all that we do." We dropped it into the prayer box.

Spirit guided us step by step along the way. When the time came for the electrical work to be done, I sat down in my recliner and began to meditate and contemplate what needed to be done. After some time in meditation, I suddenly caught a vision in my mind, and could see every-thing that needed to be done—where the receptacles needed to be and where the holes for the electrical conduit needed to be. When the vision was complete, I went out, got the supplies I needed and my drill, and I went to work.

When everything was in place, and the lines were all ready to be hooked up, I said to myself, "I really do not know what I am doing here. I do not think I want to be messing with that fuse box. I do not want to become toast. I better go take a few minutes to contemplate what I need to do." So I went back to my recliner, closed my eyes, and said, "Lord, reveal to me what needs to be revealed to me; show me what I need to be shown; guide me on what I need to do. I am listening and I await your instructions."

Then the most amazing thing happened. The doorbell rang! When I opened the door to see who it was, I saw my friend Frank from the church. He was an electrician and electrical contractor. "You know Patrick," he said, "I was driving down the street, not too far from here, and I had the strangest sense that you needed a hand with something. So I decided to stop by and check on you." He also just happened to have a new circuit breaker in his truck that would fit the requirements for my house, something he did not normally carry in his van. The work was all done in just under an hour! It was another one of the many lessons in manifestation that I received when I lived on West Hutchinson Street.

It is amazing what can happen when you allow Spirit to work for you. It is amazing what can happen when you purposely still the whirlwind of mind, in any moment, to silence its many doubts and concerns, to dissolve the obstacles it creates, and in any circumstance seek that connection with the Infinite One. As you do, you can tap into the creative potential of the universe and you will understand what it is like to be a magnet of God's good. Yes, "Thoughts held in mind do produce after their own kind; we create our reality through the thoughts we most persistently hold in mind.[14]" The only question that remains is, "What are the seed thoughts that you give your mind's energy to?" Look for the many lessons in manifestation that will come your way this week. When you see these opportunities, you will understand the best-kept secret of the ages.

I am a magnet of God's good, and I draw the abundance of the universe to me.

---

14 An Ancient Teaching that has many sources

Resources for this chapter

- <u>Foundations of Unity</u>, Unity Books, Unity Village MO

- <u>Discover the Power Within You</u>, Eric Butterworth, Harper SanFrancisco, A Division of Harper Collins Publishers, New York, NY

- Daily Inspirations, Sunday Funnies, courtesy of Christopher Chenowenthe www.positivechrisitianity.org

The Explorer

I explore the depth of my soul and I unite with my Creative potential

A minister I know recently shared with me one of his airplane experiences. He said, "I was on a plane last week, flying from Oklahoma City to LA, when we ran into some very severe turbulence. As it got worse, the passengers became more and more alarmed, and finally even the flight attendants began to look concerned.

"Finally, one of them noticed that I had 'Rev.' in front of my name on the passenger list, and so she came over to me and said, 'Sir, sir ... this is really frightening. Do you suppose you could ... I don't know ... do something, well, religious?' I thought, *'should I sing? No, read the Bible scripture? It was far too bumpy.'* So I did the next best thing; I took up a collection."[15]

Like this minister, we all have had opportunities to explore our understanding of faith and the way it moves and grows in us, prompting us to reach beyond appearance because, deep down, we know there is something greater. The explorer in you wishes to know and understand the miracles before your eyes, which only true faith can reveal. Are you willing to go there and look deeper into your experiences, to understand the mysteries that the Spirit holds in store for you? If so, affirm with me, "I explore the depth of my soul, and I unite with my creative potential."

---

15 Daily Inspirations, Sunday Funnies, courtesy of Christopher Chenowenthe www.positivechrisitianity.org

In the previous chapter, I told you about how Yvonne and I went to a prosperity workshop presented by Edwene Gaines in Chicago. Yvonne was so inspired. It had given her a vision of life she never knew existed. It was our first real glimpse of the power that can be found in applying the spiritual principles underlying the Law of Mind Action. The Law of Mind Action states, "Thoughts held in mind produce after that kind. The creative force of our mind does not differentiate between the seed of a weed, or that of a flower, it simply responds according to our most persistent seed thought, and becomes manifest in the physical world." I mean we had already toyed with these principles and learned how to manifest things like parking places and green lights. However, through this workshop with Edwene Gaines, Yvonne was able to see a way of obtaining all she wanted. She wanted to live in her own house, run her own business, and have a new car—nothing really all that grand.

Not being someone who sits around and contemplates how this all could possibility work out, waiting for life to come to her, Yvonne went right to work utilizing the principles and techniques she learned from this workshop. Sitting quietly she would visualize those things she wanted, and affirm them coming into her life. She would then take a piece of paper and write out her prayer and the vision she held in mind, always adding "… this or something better. Thank you, God." She then folded the list up and held it in her hands, seeing the light and energy of the universe flowing through it, said a heart felt prayer, and dropped her list into her prayer box. Whenever she had a thought of the house, or the business, or the new car, she would hold the thought in mind for a second, love it, bless it, and release it. Later, we took all the ideas and visions that we had for our lives and placed them on a treasure map, one of the techniques that had been shared in the thought-provoking workshop. Then, when she was prompted by Spirit to take action, she was always willing to do what she had been guided to do.

Now I already told you how we found our right and perfect home, and how we both got everything for which we had asked. I told you about a few of the things that had happened just after we had moved into our new home, but that was just the beginning of the many lessons that would unfold for us. Lessons that would stretch us and test us and lead us into deeper understanding of who we were and the path that lay before us;

lessons that would allow us to explore some of the mysteries of this realm and the various aspects of the Law of Mind Action.

About a month after moving into our new home, Yvonne received the news that Hertz Rent-A-Car would be closing their corporate location in Evanston, Illinois. This is where Yvonne worked. She had been a dedicated Hertz's employee for ten years, working most of those years at O'Hare International Airport, one of the world's busiest airports and one of Hertz's busiest locations. As you might imagine, this was a pretty insane environment at times. Yvonne dreaded the thought of going back to O'Hare to work, especially after finding solitude in what amounted to be a one-man, or should I say a one-woman, operation. She had only worked there a few months, but it had become an oasis of peace after her ten years at O'Hare. Unfortunately, the revenue generated at the location was not enough to cover its expenses. In addition, since she had chosen to bid for the Evanston location, it meant she was no longer considered part of the O'Hare workforce and if she were to go back, she would be at the bottom of the union's seniority list. She would have to work evening and graveyard shifts—shifts that experienced a great many problems.

Yvonne dreaded going back to O'Hare and contemplated her dream of opening her own business, but what would that be? She loved arts and crafts, but did not know enough about these types of businesses even to know where to begin. Therefore, she went to what she had learned from Edwene's Prosperity Workshop. She sat down in the quiet of silence and waited in a prayerful state. She asked Spirit to reveal to her the perfect opportunity to start her own business. Then she wrote her prayer out on a piece of paper, held in her hands seeing the light and energy of the universe flowing through it and dropped it her prayer box.

Now all this talk of closing the Evanston Office and Yvonne not going back to O'Hare to work was a little more than I could handle. We had just moved into a house that needed all these repairs and had a mortgage payment of over a thousand dollars of month. I just could not see how any of this was going to work. Although we did have a little money in the bank, it certainly was not enough to see us through the process of opening our own business, which may or may not bring us any money. My mind went into one of its spirals, contemplating one of its many doomsday scenarios. When I caught myself in the act, I stopped it in mid-stream, saying, "No, I won't have any more of this, cancel, cancel, cancel." I did not know what Spirit had in mind, but based on the recent past I knew, whatever it was, we would soon find out. So, I bit my tongue, watched my thoughts, and tried to hold my mind on the something great about to be revealed.

A few days after the announcement of the closing of the Evanston office, the regional manager of Hertz called Yvonne. He wanted to discuss, with Yvonne, her future working relationship with Hertz. We both thought this was very odd, that the regional manager wanted to talk to Yvonne. Although it sounded a little foreboding, it had a certain amount of intrigue. Yvonne had always been an outstanding employee at Hertz. She was normally in the top three in the sales promotions they would run for their huge staff of counter representatives. In addition, the previous year, she'd been a union rep in the collective bargaining agreement with Hertz. Something Hertz really was not prepared for; Yvonne is a very good negotiator. So Yvonne, holding the highest possible outcome in mind, thought they might want to offer her a management or a front office job.

However, that was not the reason the regional manager had set up the meeting. The Evanston office was going to be a licensee location, and they wanted Yvonne to run the office! They were offering her the opportunity to start her own business, in a joint business venture with Hertz. She would run her own office, and be completely autonomous from Hertz, while Hertz would supply the cars and pay for the office space.

At the time, it did not seem like a lot of money for the amount of work involved; however, Yvonne decided it was the best option available. The annual revenue for this location was about $200,000 dollars a year; they would pay her 15% of the total revenue for renting and cleaning the cars. However, in the first year Yvonne operated, the rental revenue doubled, then tripled, and then doubled again, until the revenue leveled off—two years later—at 1.5 million dollars a year, and her staff had grown to six people. Yvonne's personal sales touch, and the speed that she could complete transactions, not only pulled clients away from other car rental agencies in the Evanston area, but from Hertz at O'Hare, where there were always delays and minor problems. They might have to travel a little further to get their rental car from Yvonne's office, but they would be finished with their transaction in half the time and always find a smile. To top it all off, within six months of signing the licensee agreement, Yvonne was on the way to a car dealership with a much bigger down payment than either of us could have imagined for the new car she had been visualizing.

Within six months, she had manifested a house, her own business, and a new car. Apparently, this Law of Mind Action, and the techniques we were taught to control and focus our thinking really worked. Through the Power of Mind Action, and her spoken word, she had become a co-creator with Spirit to form an entirely new reality. Her most persistently held ideas and her prayers determined what was to be created. Like attracted like.

Meanwhile, all I had attracted was a house that needed a lot of repairs. I was a little overwhelmed with the speed that all this had happened, and I guess I was a little jealous. I mean, I had a four-wheel drive Subaru Brat that was pushing on six years old. It was a neat old car and I liked it, but it did not quite meet my needs at the time. So, when somebody at my courier office offered the right price for it, I sold it, and I was left to drive Yvonne's old car, which she had decided to sell herself. I guess she had just manifested the right buyer. Unfortunately, I'd never liked her old car; the seats did not fit my back comfortably. Frustrated, I became determined to put this theory to work in my life, but had to figure out what kind of car I really needed and wanted? I mean, I always loved sports cars, but thought I might need something more practical. I was always moving lots of things around, like supplies to repair the house, and I made occasional deliveries for the courier company I was working for, so I began to contemplate, and research just what type of car I needed.

The only thing I did know was that it needed to be brilliant blue, the color of the morning sky just before sunrise. You see brilliant blue is the color of faith. I was just beginning to understand that faith was the true power behind the Law of Mind Action. When I would see the Law of Mind Action being demonstrated, I would hear Jesus' words echoing in the back of my mind: "According to your faith, it will be done unto you." (Matthew 9:29) "The time is fulfilled, the Kingdom of God is at hand, turn to it and believe in the Good News." (Mark 1:15)

I realized the good news is that the creative power of this reality was within my grasp, if only I could learn how to tap into It, and direct Its energy. *Lord, help me overcome my unbelief.*

I had been like so many people who confused the word faith with belief, thinking that the words could be used interchangeably. However, they are not the same at all. Our beliefs are based on our experiences, perceptions, opinions, and a pool of worldly information that has arisen from other people's experiences, which are said to be fact. However, how often have the facts of this physical reality been proven to be incorrect? True faith helps us to look beyond our beliefs and worldly opinions, to perceive the reality of God's Kingdom and say, "Yes!" despite evidence to the contrary. Faith is an awareness, a knowing, that there is *force* working in the midst of any situation that will somehow lift us beyond the appearance, beyond the obstacles, to something greater. True faith knows no boundaries or restrictions, and can open the portals into the realm of Spirit, which produces what seem to be miracles. Faith is what told Christopher Columbus to sail across the Atlantic; it led Thomas Edison to harness electricity and the Wright Brothers to fly. Faith is what Yvonne demonstrated in holding to her vision of a house, a car, and her own business, while I had been demonstrating my belief in lack and limitation in manifesting a house that needed many repairs. We all have faith innately within us, but the question is: what do we have faith *in*? Faith is a power that needs to be called forth and developed, and I was determined to align myself with it. So the one thing I did know about my new car was that it had to be brilliant blue.

After much thought, I realized what I needed was some type of utility vehicle that I could use for my many different projects, and yet looked good as well, and would have a comfortable ride. Sports Utility Vehicles were new on the market in 1991, and only had limited sales. So I looked at, and test-drove, all the ones that were on the market: the Nissin Pathfinder, the GM Blazer and a Toyota model. The one I liked best was the Explorer. It did not have the pickup and cornering ability of the Pathfinder or Blazer, but it was a little bigger, more spacious, definitely more comfortable, and better on gas. I had made my decision, but when I went into the dealership to talk about the possibility of buying the Explorer, they did not have anything in blue—not brilliant blue or even light blue; they only came in basic colors, white, black, gray, and brown. However, they did have a really cool sports car in brilliant blue. I was caught in a dilemma; what should I do? We did not have our financing quite right; Yvonne was still making payments on her new car, and we had some big expenditures on the house to make. I decided I would wait and hold in my mind the right and perfect vehicle, manifesting at just the right time. I wrote everything down, that I wanted in my new vehicle, on a piece of paper, folded it up, held it in my hands and saw the light and energy of Spirit flowing through it, and then dropped it in my newly purchased prayer box.

One day, about six months later, I had enough of driving Yvonne's old car and decided to sell it. I put "for sale" signs in its windows and, would you believe it, the very next day someone offered me the asking price. So, I sold it right then, and it was gone, but now I had no car to drive. I had not owned my own car since I was sixteen, and had never ridden public transportation before, so I was not really sure what I would do.

I walked over to a Ford Dealership that was just a few blocks from my house, to talk with a salesman. When I told the salesman what I wanted, he walked back to his office, picked up a color chart, and pointed to the color I was describing. The color chart had just arrived that morning and it was for the next year's model of Explorers, which were about to be released.

Coincidence, I do not think so. It could not have worked with any better timing if I had ordered the color; but then … I guess I did order it. The universe has a strange way of providing our heartfelt desires, if we let go of our doubts and believe. As Jesus said, "… all things that you ask for will be given onto you if you believe." (Or you can pick one of the many other things he said, just like this)."

Well, when I told Yvonne what I was planning to do, she called the Hertz Corporate Office, who called the dealership they ordered their cars through, and were able to purchase the Explorer at just $200 over the actual dealership cost. However, they did not have any brilliant blue Explorers in stock, or on order. I would have to place a special order if I wanted that specific color. So I did, and I designed the car of my dreams: leather seats, a five speed manual transmission, and everything else I had written on my prayer request. It was the first time I had ever done that, and it felt so good. However, it would be ten weeks before it would arrive. How many of you know the date your car was made and shipped?

During that time, I would have the novelty of riding the Chicago Elevated to work and back each day, giving me the opportunity to explore one of the more unique features of Chicago, which was something I actually I decided that I liked. There was one other thing the delay in purchasing the Explorer created: the opportunity for the universe to line up all our finances. The day we picked it up, we could pay for the car with just one check. No financing was necessary. We had hit another windfall, between Yvonne's new business and just strange miraculous luck! The delay in the purchase gave us the opportunity to get a few steps ahead.

There was only one thing that both Yvonne and I had put on our treasure maps, when we'd done them a year and a half before, which had not yet manifested. But that is the topic of another day. When you ask in faith, you command the substance of the universe into action. You shape it and form it through your most persistent thoughts. Therefore, I invite you to become the explorer, and allow your mind to study the depths of your soul, so that you can unite with your creative potential and know, without a doubt, that God loves through you.

I explore the depth of my soul and I unite with my Creative potential

Resources for this chapter:

- The Twelve Powers of Man, Charles Fillmore, Unity Books, Unity Village, MO.

- Christ Enthroned, Cora Fillmore, Unity Books, Unity Village MO

- A Twelve Power Meditation Exercise, Charles Roth, Unity Books, Unity Village, MO

- Daily Inspirations, Sunday Funnies, courtesy of Christopher Chenowenthe www.positivechrisitianity.org

- The Holy Bible, NRSV

Touched by God

As I still my mind and open my heart,
I can feel the breath of the Holy Spirit flowing through me.

Some of us have had "the experience" and knew it. Others have had "the experience" and wondered what had just happened. Still others have simply dismissed "the experience" as a waking dream, an illusion, or something that could not possibly have happened. But at some point in our life, each of us will have an experience that tells us, beyond any doubt, that there is a God—that there is a Life Force present, which is greater than anything we can understand or comprehend. This experience, if we allow it, will change the way we perceive life. It can be as dramatic as the experience that rendered Paul blind, or it can be as subtle as the experience Jesus had at his baptism by John at the river. It might even occur in a quiet conversation with another. Have you ever had such an experience? Have you ever felt as if you had been "touched by God"?

I shared with you about how Yvonne and I went to this prosperity workshop presented by Edwene Gaines in Chicago, and how Yvonne was so inspired that she immediately began utilizing the tools that were shared in the workshop. Among these tools was a very clear description of the Law of Mind Action (a concept highlighted in the movie *The Secret*), special prayers and visualization techniques, a brief talk on the importance of forgiveness, and an outline for a process called treasure mapping.

Although I was somewhat resistant to any type of creative arts adventure, Yvonne and I went to work constructing our own treasure maps.

I actually found the treasure mapping process to be quite fun, and amazingly, within two years we had attracted everything we had placed on those treasure maps with the exception of one thing. We'd purchased our first house (you remember the one that needed to have everything fixed up); we each were able to purchase and pay for the car of our dreams; Yvonne had attracted her own business; and we were able to engage ourselves on our spiritual path. There was only one thing left that both Yvonne and I had put on our treasure maps that had not yet manifested—a little baby girl.

You know, thinking back on it now, I do not really know why I put that baby picture on my treasure map. Maybe it was because the baby in that picture was so cute; maybe it was because I knew that Yvonne wanted so desperately to have a baby and could not … or maybe it was just a Divine idea that Spirit planted in my mind. However, until the moment I saw that baby picture, and placed it on that treasure map, having a baby was one of the furthest things from my mind. You see, I am the third oldest in a family of nine, where everyone had to work. So, I got plenty of training changing diapers, feeding babies their formula, burping babies, and listening to them cry. I started changing diapers when I was five, and they were not the disposable kind with the Velcro strips, like we have today. What a fantastic invention that was! We used cloth diapers and pins. I can barely remember a time when I was young when I didn't have sores on my fingertips from missing the pin clasps, and pricking my clumsy little hands. In my family, you learned at a very earlier age to put a cloth over your shoulder before placing a baby on it. In my teenagers years, when I was not playing sports or working, I was baby sitting or playing peacemaker, separating my younger brothers who would never stop fighting, bickering, and teasing one another. I really do not understand how anyone raises more than two kids at a time and maintains their sanity—like Lynette on *Desperate Housewives*. I have such fond memories of my childhood. NOT! I thought I had a good understanding of the workload involved, and of the whole process of parenting. At the time, I was 37 years old. Who has their first baby at 37? However, as I held that baby picture in my hands, while constructing that treasure map, something just felt right; something had definitely shifted in me.

Later, when I looked over at Yvonne's Treasure Map, she pointed out the baby pictures she had placed on her map. I remember thinking that, if we were to have that baby girl we were envisioning, a real miracle would have to take place. Several years earlier she had gone to the doctor to inquire why she had not become pregnant after five years of marriage, and five years of trying, and had been told there was internal damage from an accident in her childhood and she would not be able to have children. Not accepting this verdict, she went to another doctor, and then another, and then another. All of them said the same thing. If we were to have children, we would have to adopt. However, the Holy Spirit had something else in mind, and was speaking to us through those pictures of babies.

A short time after the treasure mapping exercise, someone guided us to attend a weekend workshop with John Gray; the author of *Men are From Mars, and Women Are From Venus*. Dr. Gray started by explaining how men and women communicated differently, and then moved to issues that caused conflicts in relationships—issues that were anchored in childhood, which clouded our perceptions and played out in our adult relationships. Somehow, over the years, we had become the mirror images of our parents' relationships. Now that was a pretty scary image. He went on to explain how we had created these silent core beliefs that dominated everything we did. Subconsciously these parental images and core beliefs provoked our deepest fears, and set off all kinds of internal alarms. Neither of our parents had what you would call "ideal relationships." It was no wonder that Yvonne and I struggled with our own relationship. We both wanted to be anything but our parents. Through the series of workshops we took with Dr. Gray, we were able to open the way for the healing of our issues to begin. We had gained the insights necessary to be able to release the hurt and pain that resided in those old images and beliefs. In addition, we learned how to re-frame and heal them, so we could live free from their effects.

Over the next two years, we set about the forgiveness work that we had been charged to do. We would attend Dr. Gray's workshops whenever he came to Chicago. We also intensified our spiritual studies at Unity School, and began teaching Unity-based classes at our church.

Then it happened. A few months after we had manifested the last of the things placed on that treasure map, and the idea of having a baby was out of our minds, "the miracle" occurred. Yvonne announced that she was pregnant. Somehow, the doctors had been wrong, and Spirit's promptings were right. I was overwhelmed with a mixture of emotions. There was the excitement of bringing a new life into the world, the fear of the responsibility of sharing and shaping a new life, and the fear of the workload involved. I wondered how, after all Yvonne and I had been through in our own childhoods, "Could we raise a well-balanced child in our already hectic adult lives I was not certain whether or not we could pull it off.

My emotions continued to be mixed, until I was able attend a prenatal checkup with Yvonne, and heard the sound of Shavonne's heartbeat. It was one of the biggest thrills of my life; I knew right then that every-thing would be fine. A few weeks later, we got our first peek at Shavonne through the technology of ultrasound. I cannot really explain the excite-ment and intrigue I felt. At about the fifth month, I knew those electronic gadgets in the doctor's office were working; Shavonne started kicking hard enough to for me feel her tiny thumps on Yvonne's stomach.

As the final month approached, we were ready. We had taken prenatal classes and had been briefed on the different types of birth procedures and what to expect. We were ready with the breathing techniques and I was set as coach. I was also approached by two separate groups of people— Yvonne's former workmates from Hertz and a group of friends at Unity in Chicago—both wanting to give Yvonne a surprise baby shower. In the process, I was given a lesson in how wonderfully accommodating the uni-verse can be. Between the two groups, over one hundred people donated baby gifts. Just about everything we needed for Shavonne's first year was provided. I was overwhelmed with the outpouring of generosity and love.

Just after midnight, on May 30, 1992, all the signs for Shavonne's appearance into the physical world were made manifest. Yvonne had been in labor for an hour, but let me sleep a little, knowing I would prob-ably need the rest. When she called the doctor and reported her condi-tion, the doctor told her to get to the hospital as quickly as possible, as there appeared to be some complications. Although in a half state of consciousness, I managed to get myself, and most of the items we planned to take to the hospital (including Yvonne), into the car, and we were off.

When we arrived at the hospital, we were taken to what is called a birthing room. It was like a large hotel room, which could quickly and easily be converted into an operating room. Shortly after we arrived, they started hooking up monitors and IVs to Yvonne. At one point, thirteen different cords were attached to her in one way or another. The only way I could get close enough and touch her was by reaching out and touching her right knee, so much for being a breathing coach. Then we were informed that the baby was a high-risk birth, and a specialist was called. About eight a.m., the contractions increased in intensity. I knew this intuitively and did not need to watch the monitor's spike, because Yvonne almost broke my hand by squeezing it so hard. The doctors would arrive a few minutes later.

As Shavonne slowly inched her way into the world, it was as if time slowed down. A chill went through my body; I could feel Spirit's Presence so completely. In that moment, which seemed to stand still, the life and breath of the Sacred Spirit seemed to permeate the entire room in a silvery-gold aura. Every molecule within the room was woven together, connected in oneness. I could see, sense, and feel the matrix of living energy filling the room. I felt the boundaries of our individual identities drop away as the Life-Force within each of us beat with the same rhythm. Our lives were synchronized and beat with the rhythm of the Holy Spirit. The voices in the room went silent and I heard only thoughts. Despite all the people within the room, all the activity, I was calm and peace filled. I felt as if I were immersed in the Life of the Holy Spirit. In that instance, I knew, I had been touched by God! Then the miracle I know as my daughter came into the world; and I knew she had been touched by God as well. I felt the rush of the Holy Spirit pouring out upon me—God bumps, if you will, tiny little bumps running up and down my arms with a tingly little feeling that made the hair on my arms stand up. It was amazing. I felt as if I were part of the activity of the room, yet somehow separate, watching from beyond the room somewhere—watching through the eyes of God in an all-together different reality. My mind had somehow left my body.

The flurry of activity continued and, once Shavonne had completely emerged they cleaned her eyes and ears and quickly gave her a few tests. She was fine. A nurse held her up for her first picture in the outer world, which I took from across the room. Then I made my way to the other side of the room and welcomed Shavonne to this world. She looked up and recognized me, as one of the voices that had been talking to her for the past several months. She smiled. My heart melted. As I looked at her beautiful blue eyes, I saw pure Spirit; I saw the Holy Spirit shining forth.

The Apostle Paul wrote, "There is but one body and one Spirit ... one God and Father who is above all and through all and in all." (Ephesians 4:4 – 6) I felt this one Spirit. The sacred energy of life flows in all things. With each breath, we breathe in the Holy Spirit's Presence and it flows throughout our being. It is etched into our very DNA, and yet how often do we realize it? In that moment, one that is forever etched in memory, I looked into Shavonne's eyes for the very first time and I saw the stirring of the Sacred Spirit. I caught a glimpse of our truest nature as children of God. I saw and felt the one Spirit that blazes in each and every one of us.

It is no wonder that, from his illuminated mind and heart, Jesus said, "The time is fulfilled, the Kingdom of God is at hand, turn to it and believe in the Good News." (Mark 1:15) It is right here, right now; it is all around us. If only we would awaken like that prodigal one, and make the decision to rise up and return home. All we need do is seek Its Presence. Is that not what Jesus continually advised us to do? "In all things seek first the Kingdom, and Its harmony." (Matthew 6:25 Aramaic version)[16] In all things seek first Love's presence.

Remember Paul's words in Acts 17:28 "... they would search for God and perhaps even grope for God ... though indeed God is not far from each one of us, for in God we live, move, and have our being" (Acts 17:28)." The Sacred Spirit is not far from us. It is only as far as our next breath. We only need to seek its presence to know it: in a baby's eyes, in a loving embrace, or in your neighbor's cry for help. A divine matrix of life surrounds, enfolds, and connects us with all of life. If we are to evolve beyond our current dwelling place in our mortal minds, and reach our true potential, we need to stretch our awareness to feel its presence. The

---

16 The Prayers of The Cosmos, Neil Douglas- Koltz, Harper and Row Publishers, San Francisco, New York, NY, page 57

Sacred Spirit is not simply what can be seen and felt through our physical senses; It is an ocean of moving energy, and its invisible vibration creates and gives expression to all of life.

Many years ago, the miracle I call Shavonne came into the world, and I was left in awe at the wonder that life is. In fact, it mystifies me. The activity of Sacred Spirit is not always felt or seen in dramatic ways; sometimes it will be felt in quiet conversation or music that touches the soul. However, at some point in each of our lives, we all have an experience that tells us, beyond any doubt, that there is a God—that there is a Life Force present, which is greater than anything we can understand. This experience, if we allow it, will change the way we perceive life. We will know that we have been touched by God, and we will be forever changed. Therefore, I invite you to begin seeking the Presence of the Infinite One. As you do, you will know without a doubt that the God loves you.

As I still my mind and open my heart,
I can feel the breath of the Sacred Spirit flowing through me.

Resources for this talk:

- <u>What You Can Feel You Can Heal, A Guide for Enriching Relationships,</u> John Gray, Ph.D., Heart Publications, Mill Valley CA

- <u>Men Are From Mars, Women Are From Venus,</u> John Gray, Ph.D., Harper Collins, New York, NY

- <u>The Secret,</u> *the movie,* 2006, Prime Time Productions

- <u>The Prayers of The Cosmos,</u> Neil Douglas- Koltz, Published Harper and Row Publishers, San Francisco, New York, NY

- <u>The Holy Bible, New Revised Standard Version</u>

Breaking Through

Empowered by the Christ Spirit, I break through all that limits me.

Daytime soap operas are a pretty good example of how some people go through life. The characters on some of these television shows seem to repeat the same cycles in their life over and over again, rarely catching a glimpse of their true character, which lies deep within them, and rarely understanding why they are doomed to draw the same type of struggles and conflicts into their lives. We have the same tendency to repeat the dramas and challenges of *our* lives, carrying them from one person to the next, and then on to the next. We might moan, whine, and complain about them, because breaking through these cycles—and the ingrained beliefs that promote them—can be very difficult. In order to do so we must be able to recognize them for what they are, and be motivated and willing to let them go, while visualizing ourselves on the other side of challenges, free and clear of the devastating effects that they might have.

Breaking through these repetitive cycles and ingrained beliefs is similar to breaking a board with your hand, as they do in a Karate demonstration. We all have the ability do it, but we have to have the desire, the willingness, and the ability to see our hand moving *through* the board to a point *beyond* the board. It is critical to be able to imagine—to see—the end result in our mind before we begin. Otherwise, we will fall short. As we engage our imagination, it links with this incredible matrix of energy and life that surrounds us and pulls our hand to the point in space beyond the board, to the point we have imagined.

A few years ago, I went to workshop at Unity Village, titled "Breaking Through." Silently, I had always wondered whether or not I could break a one-inch board, at least without breaking my hand at the same time. As a result of the workshop facilitator's demonstration, and the energy and enthusiasm it created in the participants, I dropped my reservations about trying to break a board, and I tried it. On my first attempt, I engaged my imagination very well, feeling—and then seeing—my hand moving through the board. Then I shattered the board, almost knocking the person holding the board down. However, my ego did not get way out of control, as I thought it might, because when I looked around everyone was breaking boards. If the board wasn't shattered on the first attempt, it shattered on the second. Some of these participants were very small, with very little muscle, and some others were not what you would call spring chickens. As I watched the boards breaking, I realized this demonstration was really simply a matter of physics, and seeing the world through a slightly different perspective.

I have also realized that this is the same type of physics that allows us to put a straw through a potato. It is simply a matter of physics. In fact, I realized it might even be easier to break a board, than to put a straw through a potato. Which do you think would be easier? You might ask, "How can you put a flimsy straw through such a solid mass as a potato?" However, anyone can do it through the art known as Potato Karate. I learned the art at the Museum of Science and Industry in Columbus, Ohio. It works on the same principle of physics as breaking through one-inch board. It is just a matter of seeing our world and the laws of nature a little differently.

If you doubt this idea, you can take the time to do it yourself. It does not really matter what type of potato. However, you might like to get a straw from McDonalds or Sonic; they have good, sturdy straws. Holding the potato, get a firm grip on the upper end of the straw. Then visualize the straw going through the potato to a point two or three inches beyond the potato. Then one … two … three … act with abandon, no holding back, no jerking back. If you can move into action without doubt or holding back, the straw will go through the potato and out the other side. This can be a truly amazing exercise.

The imagination, combined with the power of faith, plays a powerful role in this exercise. The imagination is actually the movement of the universal mind flowing through us; it creates an inner picture that allows us to shape and form the substance of the invisible ethers just beyond the realm of our sight. The imagination is that part of us that allows us to create an image of ourselves standing on the other side of any obstacles we face. The only question remaining is this: "Where do you allow your imagination to play in fields of doubt and fear, or in the fields of possibilities, life and Spirit?" Take, for example, a fire walk. You can stare at the hot coals and will yourself across them, but if you simply rely on your willpower, you will probably end up with severe burns. However, if you imagine yourself surrounded and enfolded by Spirit— divinely protected—being transported by Spirit and impervious to the heat of the coals, you will walk across the coals unscathed. Your imagination can take you places your intellect thinks impossible.

We can break through our self-limiting thoughts and beliefs, in much the same way. We follow the same principle we use when breaking through a board or putting a straw through a potato. It is just a matter of physics. When we find ourselves standing before an obstacle, we need to see ourselves being filled with the Sacred Breath of Life, and feeling the life of the Divine flowing through us—while holding the end result in our minds. As we do, the imagination links with the invisible matrix of energy and life, to carry us to the point we have envisioned. As we let go of our doubt and fears, the Sacred Breath of Life will bring us to where only our imagination can see us being.

A few chapters ago, I told you about the first time someone told me I would make a good minister. It was way back in 1987, when I'd just started taking classes on metaphysics at Unity in Chicago. At that time, I had never given a thought to being a minister, in fact I could not even conceive of it. So I just looked at them rather oddly and laughed, "Who me? You have got to be kidding."

The truth is that I had developed a great fear of public speaking. My voice would quiver, and my legs would shake. Sometimes I was so panicked about being in front people. Like at my own wedding, when I opened my mouth the only thing that would come out was air. This very intense fear arose from childhood experiences, when I would stand up to read in middle school and would read the text backwards. It was not intentional. In fact, I did not even understand I was doing it, but I would do it over and over again. The other kids thought I was making fun and would laugh, and the teacher would become angry. I did not understand why; it was both bewildering and embarrassing! I did not know that I was dyslexic, and neither did anyone else; they had not yet discovered that it was a learning disability.

You can imagine how I dreaded reading aloud. As a result, I became terrified of doing *anything* in front of people. I remember one speech class in college, when I stood at the lectern with all my note cards in order, trying to contain my nervousness and fears, when my words froze in mid-sentence. I was shaking so hard that I dropped all the cards on the floor. The class burst out with a roar of laughter, and the teacher released his frustration on me! I would learn about dyslexia the next year in college, when I was taking an early childhood development class for my degree in psychology.

Jesus said, "Come to terms quickly with your adversary while you are on the way to court with him, or your adversary may hand you over to the judge, and the judge to the guard, and you will be thrown into prison. Truly I tell you, you will never get out until you have paid the last penny (Matthew 5:25-26)." You know, the first time I read this passage I thought, *"How can this be fair?"*

However, Jesus was not saying that your adversary already has the deck stacked against you down at the courthouse. What he was saying is that, when we have an adversarial thought, a thought that causes a negative or fearful reaction, we need to settle with it and dispose of the thought quickly. If we do not work through the fear, our own judging faculty will hand us over to the jailor called *fear*—where we will serve our sentence chained to this negative, limited belief. We will not escape from this self-created prison until we have paid every last penny, that is, until we have worked through every feeling related to that negative belief. I had become a prisoner of my fears. In this instance, I had become a prisoner of my fear of public speaking, and my fear of how dyslexia might show up and disrupt my life. Consequently, I learned to play it safe and to stay in the realm of my own restricted and limited understanding.

However, a very strange thing happens when you commit yourself to pursuing the path of Spirit. Spirit moves you into a position to break through your fears, whether or not you think you are ready. The same year in which that person made that very strange statement to me, about becoming a minister, I was returning to my home church from a Spiritual Education and Enrichment Retreat at Unity Village, and I decided to ask one of my ministers why the church did not teach more Unity-based classes. I remember Sara's smile, as she pulled a book out from somewhere beneath her desk and handed it to me. "You know Patrick," she said, "that is not something Mike and I have time to do. But we would like you to consider teaching a class about this book when we move into our new facility on Thome (a street on the far north side of Chicago)." My mind raced, *"But, but ...,"* and my words froze. I did not know how to tell her that I could not stand in front of people and speak. You know what I found myself doing in just three short months? Although I still could not see myself being a minister, teaching had always been something that tugged at my heart. I had always envisioned teaching kids though, rather than adults, and a subject that I actually knew something about, like football or history or math.

I surrendered to the task that the Sacred Spirit had laid before me, saying, "Guide me to what I need to do. Reveal to me what needs to be revealed; guide me to what I must do." The first thing I was guided to do was join a Toastmaster's Group, which would teach me about the basics of constructing, and giving, a talk. Toastmasters also helped me to visualize a point in my life where I would be free of the paralyzing fear, and be able to speak unrestricted and with confidence. Although, I still had to break through the ingrained belief that held that fear in place. I held the images of my past speaking and reading experiences in my mind, and declared to myself over and over again, "These images are not the truth of who I am. The experiences that led to my disability have no power over the truth of who I am, a child of God." I declared, "The Sacred Breath of Life will guide my words as I express myself easily, effectively, and joyously in all matters."

Well, it mostly worked. The first series of classes that Yvonne and I taught were in 1989, after just a few sessions with our Toastmaster's group. The class was held in the fellowship hall of our new building on Thome. However, the fellowship hour seemed to last a lot longer than normal that afternoon, and at one o'clock, when the class was supposed to begin, the area in which we were supposed to have the class was still full. We asked everyone who was not staying for the class to please move to another part of the grounds. But, no one left. Over 100 people stayed. So, Yvonne and I pulled up a chair to lean against, seized our chaotic energy, breaking through our fears, and began.

Guy Lynch, a Unity minister says, "Fear is not the enemy. Fear is your friend. But, you have to transform it. Fear is the Sacred Breath of Life speaking through you, to point out the area of your needed growth. So step through the fear with all your heart."[17]

When you have a fearful reaction in your life, stop and recognize it for what it is. Ask yourself if there is indeed a reason to be fearful, or is the fear really related to events buried in your subconscious. Then engage your imagination to take you to a point beyond your fear. As we surrender our fears to the Sacred Spirit, our awareness expands, and we realize that what we have feared was merely an illusion. We might then realize that the word "fear" is really an acronym: False Evidences Appearing Real—or as my wife, Yvonne, says, *"Frightening Experiences causing us to Avoid Real issues within our self."*

However, there are times when we cannot clearly articulate the fear or belief that is creating a barrier in our life. The year before I applied for ministerial school, I had gotten to the point where I felt I could not squeeze one more thing into my head. I was overwhelmed, I did not feel life was working right and I did not want to learn anything new. Although I resisted, Yvonne insisted that we go to the Unity Village in an attempt to complete our licensed teacher certificates. So when I found myself sitting in a prayer class at Unity Village, I asked, "Dear lord, why do I feel this way? Reveal to me what needs to be revealed. What is blocking my desire to learn? Why am I feeling out of harmony with all I have come to love?

---

17 Words Spoken by Guy Lynch at a Intensive for Ministerial Student at Unity School of Christianity 1996

Reveal to me what needs to be revealed." Then I held a vision of myself feeling free and unrestricted.

My next class was the History of Christianity, and we watched a film. There was a point in the film, where they showed a series of images that went from one Catholic Cathedral to another and then to another and another. They were all ancient, and beautiful, and were Cathedrals from all around the world. They were all filled with people on their knees preparing for communion, striking their chests, and saying, "Lord, I am not worthy!" The way the film clip was shown people repeated the phrase over and over and over again. My mind shot back to when I was child, kneeling in church, proclaiming those same words, "Lord, I am not worthy," over and over again. Tears filled my eyes. I could not stop crying. Suddenly, I understood why I'd been feeling the way I'd been feeling. I understood why I had always felt so unworthy, and why my life would seemingly break apart after achieving a measure of success.

After six years of attending Catholic schools, and attending Catholic Mass six days a week, I had probably heard this phrase, just before hitting my heart Chakra, more than a thousand times. It had silently programmed my mind, very powerfully, with this core belief that would dominate my life for decades. Unfortunately, I never really heard the second part of the phrase: "Simply say the words and I shall be healed." This is a very powerful phrase, in and of itself, but I had never heard it. This realization explained so much, and why, despite all that I had been learning in Unity, there were times I felt so disconnected and unworthy. There was this silent programming from my past that seemed to be running my life.

In breaking through the barriers that we have created in our awareness, we begin to see and feel things that we have never seen or felt before; we are freed to think in a whole new way. To break through the cycles and ingrained beliefs that seem to be dominating our life, we need to be motivated and willing to let them go, while visualizing ourselves on the other side of challenges—free and clear of the devastating effect that they might have. Surrender to the activity of the Sacred Breath of Life and allow the Infinite One to guide you to the incredible place of your dreams.

"Empowered by the Sacred Breath of Life, I break through all that limits me."

Resources for this chapter:

- *Breaking Through*, Leadership Development Workshop presented by Brian Biro

- *Potato Karate*, the Museum of Science and Industry in Columbus Ohio

- Unity Ministerial Education Program, notes from a lecture given by Rev. Guy Lynch in 1996

- The Holy Bible, NRSV

Seventy Times Seven – Means It's A Process

I release and I let go, and I allow God's love to flow.

Some time ago, I learned a very valuable lesson. I found myself in a heated argument with a coworker. I was right. She was wrong, and I was going to prove it. When work ended, I went home carrying my bag of resentment. The drive home was miserable, and I caught every red light. When I arrived home, I relived the entire miserable experience for my wife. I could not eat, and then I could not sleep. When I arrived at work the next morning, I was ready to pick up the fight. Only my co-worker was too busy to notice my anger. She was sharing with everyone the wonderful evening she'd had. When she'd arrived home after work the day before, her husband had surprised her by taking her out to a five-star French restaurant. Then they went dancing, and to top it all off, he gave her a pair of diamond-studded earrings.

I thought, *"What kind of justice is this? Whatever happened to karmic debt?"* It was in that moment when I realized that my holding onto anger and resentment did not affect her at all! It had only hurt *me,* and ruined *my* evening. She was off having a grand time, while I was imprisoned by my own resentment. I learned a valuable lesson that day.[18]

How often do we recognize what lurks behind our irritations? Now, I had a perfect right to my annoyance. I was right and she was wrong. However, as I thought about it, I realized my anger came out of fear—the

---

18 Thoughts and Insights of Yvonne McAndrew, unpublished works

fear that I might not get something I wanted, which in this case was the acknowledgment that I was right. As I paused and looked within, a shift in my consciousness occurred. It was a huge shift. In that moment of reflection, I chose to open the doorway to God's Kingdom, by choosing to follow the path of forgiveness.

Many times, throughout each day, we are giving the opportunity to choose between the path of forgiveness and love or the path of blame and resentment. Blame and resentment is a path that separates us from the experience of God's Kingdom of good, and what we truly seek in life.

Emmet Fox wrote, "When you hold resentment against someone, you are bound to that person by a cosmic link, a real—though mental— chain. You are tied by a cosmic link to the thing that you hate. The one person in the whole world whom you dislike the most is the very one to whom you are attaching yourself, by a hook that is stronger than steel. Is this what you wish?" [19] The moment you begin resenting a person, you become their slave. They control your dreams, and your waking hours. You allow them to rob you of your peace of mind and goodwill, and that takes away the pleasure of your work, play, and fun. You cannot take a vacation without them going along! So, if you want to be a slave, harbor your resentments. However, if you want to know peace, joy, and happiness, forgiveness is the key. You cannot "serve two masters." You cannot hold in mind thoughts of love and anger at the same time, nor can you experience peace and happiness as long you hold onto your resentments and feelings that you need to be right. You must choose, and based on your choice, you determine how you will experience the world.

Jesus said, "Come to terms with your adversary quickly," or your anger, your hurt, and your pain will hold you in bondage. "Come to terms quickly" before you go to the judge, the judge of self-righteousness—you know the rationalization: "I am right and she is wrong and I am going to make her pay." Come to terms with your anger and resentment before you become the judge and the jury, or you will find that you are the one who has been imprisoned—imprisoned by your own thoughts. And, "… you will not get out until you have given forth every last bit." (Matthew 5:25-26, NRSV)

---

19 The Sermon on the Mount, The Key to Success in Life, Emmet Fox, Harper Collins, New York, NY.

Forgiveness is such a simple concept, and yet it is so hard to implement into our thinking and our life. Why? Because when we feel that someone has harmed us, we feel that we have every right to demand justice! It is the American way! We think, *"They are the ones that are going to have to pay up and apologize; after all, they were wrong and I was right."* And, we probably *were* right. We are perfectly entitled to the way we feel and we may be perfectly justified, but at what price? We have to ask ourselves, "How is our anger, hurt, and pain serving us?" The longer we hold onto that negative emotional energy, the more it poisons us and builds barriers in our minds and hearts to the very goodness we are seeking. Unknowingly, we communicate this negative emotional energy out to others around us, and guess what happens? They respond to it. It soon becomes impossible to escape the escalating nature of the negativity we have sown. It is so perplexing. We see this anger, resistance, and hostility everywhere, but this is because the people around us are reflecting back to us what we feel inside, and have projected out to them. Unfortunately, we seldom do make that connection.

Sometimes we try to hide or deny our angry feelings by stuffing them down. We think that we can avoid dealing with them that way. We all have seen it. We will say something to someone that unknowingly pushes their buttons and they get upset. We can see it in their eyes and mannerism and so we will ask them what is bothering them. They respond,

"Nothing," they respond, "Ain't nothing wrong with me!"

"Uh huh."

You cannot hide your anger and resentment; it is like trying to hide a piece of broccoli in a glass of milk. You remember trying to do that when you were a kid? The green always shows up, bumping against the outside of the glass, always showing up somewhere. [20]

Stop and think for a moment about an event that has really challenged your sense of what is right and wrong. You may have wanted to do the "Christian" thing and forgive them, but sometimes that can be really hard. We all have had things done to us, and to those we love, that we think are unforgivable, and we really want them to pay. Then a present-day event triggers one of our hidden buttons, which triggers some related

---

20 Stories and Insights of Yvonne McAndrew, unpublished

memories. Pretty soon, we are reliving those old experiences we thought we had put behind us. Consequently, we experience the pain and anger of that suppressed memory over and over again.

The truth is that a deeper understanding of forgiveness is essential to our spiritual growth and unfoldment, and necessary for our physical well-being and happiness. One day, when Jesus was teaching, the topic of forgiveness came up and Peter, wanting further explanation of what he had just heard, asked Jesus, "Rabbi, if another member of the church sins against me, how often should I forgive? As many as seven times?" Jesus responded, "Not seven times, but, I tell you, seventy times seven (Matthew 18:21)."

The number seven was a mystical number in ancient Judaism, which represented physical fullness and completion, and often referred to an unspecified number of steps in the process of completion of any given subject. There are seven days in a week, and seven days in the story of Creation. In the book of Revelation, there are seven churches, seven seals, and seven trumpets, each of which represented the end of a particular process. *Seventy times seven* represents completeness multiplied tenfold and then multiplied once again by the fullness of forgiveness. In other words, *seventy times seven* implies unlimited forgiveness. When you feel you have completed all the forgiveness work on an issue that you think you can do, you still have work to do. *Seventy times seven* means it is a process; forgiveness is an ongoing and continual process.

I learned all about the nature of this ongoing process of forgiveness my first year in ministerial school. The ministerial program was actually designed to engage "the process;" the process of personal growth and development; the process of opening up the unhealed wounds buried deep within our subconsciousness; the process of....

We would open these old wounds so that we could forgive, release, and heal them; so we might be clearer channels through which Spirit could express itself; and so we would be better ministers.

Around "The Village," they simply call it "processing." Sounds like something you do to milk when it is changed into cheese, not something you do to people. (Although at times during this process, I really did feel more like cheese than a person).

Now, I had been through the process of self-discovery before, so I thought, *"Here we go again. Been there, done that, got the T-shirt, and don't want it no more."* I really did not believe that there was anything else to find. But the forgiveness process is similar to peeling away layers of an onion. You keep finding new layers to peel away, until you finally get down to the core. Then you can look at these core issues, and begin to understand why you react to certain things the way you do. Like when my wife would go out and buy a new outfit, a sense of panic used to overcome me. I would yell, "How are we ever going to afford that?" These were words I often heard coming out of my father's mouth when I was growing up. Yvonne would respond, "That's just money and trust issues, don't you think?"

Through the exercises involved in the forgiveness process, we would get to a point where it was possible to comfortably deal with the issues that arose. However, once the pain dissolves, you find a new freedom.

My core issue was that I did not feel I was worthy: worthy of love, success or happiness. Deep within my subconscious, there remained a seed of the belief from my religious upbringing that said, "I am here on earth to suffer." No matter how good I was, or how hard I tried, I could never be good enough. The more I suffered, the better chance I had to get into heaven. So, anytime I would achieve a degree of love, happiness, or success, I would find a way to short circuit the achievement. I would not even think about asking for help. I would just have to suffer and endure the pain. I did not trust anyone to support me, because they were sure to fail. God could never love me, because I just was not good enough.

I will never forget the day I received the envelope for acceptance into Unity's Ministerial Education Program. I thought it was just an honor to be invited to the Unity Village for the interviews. I thought I had a good background with my local Unity church, but I looked around the Fillmore Chapel and saw so many qualified people. I wondered, "How could they choose just twenty-five out of the group?" I began to doubt. *"Am I worthy?"*

When they handed out the envelopes, I waited on pins and needles; the direction of my life depended upon it. Of course, I received my envelope near the end of the process. The dread of rejection hung over me. Therefore, I chose to wait for the last few envelopes to be handed out before I opened mine. A number of people were still in the chapel, waiting to open their envelope as well. We all counted to three and then opened our envelopes at the same time.

When I opened my letter, I read, "It is the decision of the committee," And I thought, *"We all know what that phrase means."* and I stopped reading. Immediately, I thought I was redirected (which was what they called *not getting in*), and accepted the verdict. I was not good enough. Something told me to read the letter again. Once again, I read, "It is the decision of the committee," and although I had been studying and teaching Truth principles, and working on my forgiveness issues rigorously for nine years, deep down inside, I still had a grain of that core belief that I was not worthy.

Fortunately, when Yvonne read the letter, she got really excited. I looked at her and thought, *"Why is she jumping up and down in her seat?"* Then she said, "Look at me," and pointed to the letter. "Keep reading. You're in!" When I read the letter for the third time, I kept reading. "It is the decision of the committee that Patrick K. McAndrew be accepted ... "

I was accepted! I was worthy of acceptance into ministerial School! That is when that embedded seed-belief really became threatened and cried out, "Did they really know what they were doing?" Did I know what I was doing? *"Oh my God, what have I done?"* All my old self-limiting beliefs stepped forward, from deep within my subconscious, to challenge and try to sabotage this opportunity. I could think of a hundred and one reasons why I should not attend ministerial school, and they all had to do with fear, feelings of unworthiness, and unprocessed, restrictive core beliefs.

Most of us have some type of restrictive core beliefs that limit and tint the way we see the world, and it creates all kinds of turmoil. We pick up these limiting beliefs from a variety of sources: our parents, teachers, friends, and traumatic experiences. Because we hold these beliefs at some level of our being, we draw experiences into our life that reinforce these restrictive beliefs, and now they tend to dominate everything we do—just as I had already made up my mind that I was not worthy of getting into ministerial school.

Even if we have done forgiveness work, there are times these phantom, limiting beliefs peek out of their hiding place to test us. If we do not deal with them, eventually our lives become so unbearable they explode, and our life crumbles. We need to look at them squarely and say, "I recognize you, you untrue thoughts. I release you, and I let you go, and allow God's love to flow."

In my lowest moments of processing this worthiness issue, a portal into the Kingdom opened up and I caught glimpses of what lies beyond the pain of my past. In some of my darkest moments, Shavonne, who was four at the time, would come in and, without prompting or reason, wrap her arms around me and say, "Daddy, I love you." Invariably her smile, laughter, and love would remind me of the beauty that I have within me—a beauty that I had not realized. If this special divine creature could love me so freely and passionately, I must be worthy of love. I knew that God had brought her into my life to show me that I am worthy of love, success, and happiness.

The humorous thing about forgiveness is that people think forgiveness is for the other person. Forgiveness is not saying that a certain behavior, or what someone might have done, is acceptable or that we need to be a doormat so that others can walk all over us. Forgiveness does not mean forgetting. When we withhold forgiveness, thinking we are punishing someone else, we hold onto our own guilt, anger, and resentments. It is like placing a veil of darkness between our Spirit and our soul. This negativity prevents us from experiencing the activity of Spirit. As the veil darkens, from other negative experiences, our lives become more and more difficult, and we suffer illness, disease, and poverty. Little by little, bit-by-bit, we store this toxic energy throughout our minds and bodies. We cloud the vision of our perception with a dark veil of negativity, and cannot see the world clearly, which I think is the original concept behind the word that was translated as "sin."

Forgiveness is the key to living fully. It unlocks the chains of negativity that bind us and releases all that weighs us down, easing our burden so we can catch the current of life, and soar to our potential. Forgiveness literally means to give forth, and has little to do with the traditional idea of repentance or letting someone off the hook for a perceived misdeed. Forgiveness is not for someone else; it is for us, so that we can give forth and release the hurts, pains, resentments, and anything else that might be creating hardship in our lives. It disconnects the buttons that we have hardwired to our emotional fuse box, and is complete only when we can mentally recall an event, or person, without experiencing the negative emotional charge that went with it. The reality is that forgiveness constitutes a mental bath—washing away things that can poison us. This practice of mental cleansing frees us. Like a shower in the morning, it wakes us up and it makes us feel alive.

Seventy times seven means it's a process; forgiveness is an ongoing and continual process that will open the portal of our minds to the Infinite One's ever-expanding Kingdom of good, which lies just beyond our view.

I release, and I let go, and I allow God's love to flow.

Resources:

- <u>Stories and Insights of Yvonne McAndrew,</u>

- <u>The Sermon on the Mount</u>, Emmet Fox, Harper Collins, New York, NY

- <u>Prayers of the Cosmos, Translations of the Aramaic Words of Jesus,</u> Neil Douglas-Koltz, Harper and Row San Francisco, New York NY

- <u>Metaphysical Bible Dictionary,</u> Charles Fillmore, Unity Books, Unity Village, MO

- <u>Discover the Power Within You</u>, Butterworth, Harper and Row San Francisco, New York, NY

- <u>The Revealing Word,</u> Charles Fillmore, Unity Books, Unity Village, MO

- <u>Webster's New World Dictionary,</u> Warner Books

- <u>The Holy Bible, New Revised Standard Version</u>

Life is Like Floating

As I trust the sea of life to support me,
I realize that I am floating on the breath of the Infinite!

Wow! The Oklahoma summers can be scorching hot. One evening I was out in front of my house at around ten o'clock, watering my lawn, and it still was more than 90 degrees. When I stepped out onto the concrete street in my bare feet, for just a moment, I could still feel the heat from the day coming up through my feet. When water hit the street, steam came pouring up around me. When it really gets hot like that, there is nothing more refreshing than diving into a pool of cold, clear water. You can literally feel the stress of the heat melt away.

Are you a swimmer? Now, I do not mean the type of swimming where you go over to the pool or the lake, stick your foot in the water, and go, "Oooh," when it's cold. I mean, are you someone who goes to the pool and immerses your whole self in the water? I love swimming, and floating provides me with an overwhelming sense of peace. It reminds me that life is like floating on the breath and substance of God. When I am floating, I have such a feeling of serenity, harmony and tranquility.

Looking up, I see the deep blue sky, decorated with a few soft, white, fluffy clouds; the water muffles the only sounds I hear. I can relax and watch the movement of the sky, and the activity going on about me, or I can close my eyes and drift in the comforting support of the water. If I struggle or fight, I will sink. I need do nothing but allow the water to support me as I drift on the surface. At some point, I become one with the water and all that surrounds me. Floating provides a perfect state for meditation and for experiencing the feeling of oneness.

Once upon a time, I swam up to two miles, three times a week, so I consider myself to be a very good swimmer. I started swimming when I was three, and at five began swimming competitively. However, for many years, as hard as I tried, I simply could not float. I guess that is why I continued to fail at floating, because I tried hard, and it is not about trying hard; it is about trusting, and letting go of the need to *do* something! I did not trust the water to support me. I felt I needed to do something to maintain myself on the water's surface. Sure enough, the harder I tried, the more quickly I would sink. To experience the joy and peace of floating in a pool, lake, or ocean, you need only relax and trust the water to support you! I was amazed to find out even infants and small children float naturally, if they are placed in the water by their parents.

I have even heard tales of toddlers who have fallen into the pool to be found by their parents floating face up, safe and sound. Amazing! They instinctively trust the water to support them. It is not until they grow a little older, and begin to develop fears of the water, that they find it hard to float on the water's surface.

For me, life is like floating. The key is in trusting the sea of life to support me, which, believe it or not, It is designed to do. However, this concept of trust has been very difficult for me to understand. I must say I have been given many opportunities to learn it! This idea of trust contradicts much of what I learned growing up. Do you remember hearing phrases like this: "If you expect to make anything of yourself, you have to work really hard and be really lucky." "If you want something done right, you have to do it yourself." "Life is hard, and then you die." "No pain, no gain."

These were phrases I heard all the time! Consequently, I developed the belief that life was hard and that, if I really wanted something, I could count only on myself to do it; I could not trust anyone or anything and that, my friend, is a very lonely existence! I have often felt like I must do something to support myself, to stay afloat on the turbulent sea called "life." However, the harder I tried, and the more I struggled to stay afloat, the more I would get that sinking feeling. You see, life is like floating, and I did not trust the Sea of Life, or anyone else, to support me.

After a long day of teaching, Jesus sent the disciples across the Sea of Galilee, while he stayed behind to pray. But, the boat was slowed by contrary winds, and tossed by the waves, so Jesus went to them, walking across the water. When Peter saw him, he called out, "Lord, command me to come to you on the water." When Jesus beckoned, Peter climbed out of the boat and began to walk, but halfway there he was distracted by the wind and waves, and started to sink, crying out for help. Immediately, Jesus went to his rescue, reaching out his hand to catch him and said, "You of little faith, why did you doubt?" (Matthew 14:22 – 33)

Why do we doubt? Why? In this physical reality, there is much that tells us to do so: the television, the news, well-meaning friends and family. Yet Spirit beckons to us to walk out on the Sea of Life, but in order to do so, we must let go of our doubts and fears, and trust the infinite oneness. Peter eventually learned how to trust Spirit to support him, and so can we. If we study Peter's words and actions in the New Testament, we see that this trust in Spirit developed over time, as his awareness of the spiritual dimension developed—just as I learned over time to trust the water in a pool to support me. It has taken me quite some time, and many lessons, to truly understand this concept—that life is like floating—but I think I finally have the hang of it.

As I shared in an earlier chapter, I remember the very first time that someone told me I would be a good minister! At that time, I simply could not conceive of it. I had developed a great fear of public speaking, and because of that fear, I had long before given up the idea of seeking any type of employment, that would require me to get up in front of people and speak. Yet, deep down in my heart, I had always wanted to be a teacher of some sort. However, for some mysterious reason, people continued to tell me they thought I would make a good minister. They definitely saw something in me that I did not see in myself. It was Spirit moving through them, beckoning me to step out on the sea of life. Finally, after a number of people made this comment, I started to think, *"Hmm, well I don't know, but maybe it might be possible to teach a class at the church; I'd like to try that."* Spirit quietly guided me to the steps I needed to take to accomplish that goal. Let's just say I had some definite fears to overcome first.

When I started teaching classes at Unity in Chicago way back 1989, it gave me a sense of satisfaction I had never experienced. After a while, teaching was all I wanted to do, and entering the ministry was the only way I could satisfy that desire. However, I could not see how that could happen. I would have to leave my job and my wonderful home, which I had just finished remodeling, and move from Chicago to Kansas City. How could I manage going to school full time and support my family? If I were going to go to school, how could I give it my full attention, if I worked a full-time job? From whatever angle I approached it; it just did not make any logical sense. Then, there was that self-doubt; I doubted my ability and my self-worth.

Finally, I was prompted by this inner knowing that I should apply to ministerial school, so I did. In my mind, I really did not think that it was something that I could do, but by this time, I had learned to follow the voice of my intuition, and to take the steps Spirit guided me to take. Yet, even after I applied for ministerial school and went for the interviews, I did not believe I would be accepted. I looked around and saw so many candidates who were so much more qualified than I was; but I figured I did not have anything to lose. I simply did the best I could, letting go of the results, and allowing Spirit to direct me. I just did it. I acted on faith and took one step at a time, allowing the chips to fall where they may—trusting Spirit to support me in the process, and knowing that, if this was what I was supposed to do, the right doors would open.

Even after I was accepted into ministerial school, I really did not think there was any way I could afford to go through with it. The more I was able to slow my mind's monkey chatter down, the better able I was to hear the inner knowing. Finally, about two months before school started, I knew that I was on the right path. That is when my boss, unaware of my plans to go to ministerial school, walked in and announced that I had earned a promotion and a huge raise. The raise and promotion was something that I had wanted for a very long time; in a way, it was the answer to my prayers. The raise and promotion would solve many questions I had about my lifestyle and my security—at least if I did not go to ministerial school. Quite ironically, it was that offer that convinced me of what I needed to do, which was to go to school. I came to the awareness that God was my source, not my job, and the Infinite One would provide the financial means for me to go to ministerial school if that was indeed my calling.

A few weeks later, as I was preparing to make the move from Chicago to Kansas City, I found myself in a sense of panic. We had been focused on getting our house in Chicago ready to sell, and had put off finding a place to live until that was done—very logical, right? Now, it was just five weeks before school was scheduled to start, and my wife and I had decided to take Memorial Day weekend to go to Kansas City to look for a place to live. I hurried home from work at about two p.m., to get the car loaded for the trip, but something did not seem right. When we were all ready to get on the road, Yvonne said, "Now, don't get upset." You know that just the way she said that made my anxiety levels go up. She said, "I have this feeling we are not suppose to go to Kansas City this weekend."

I looked at her in surprise, and replied, "I have the same feeling."

We did something very strange that day. We listened to our intuition, and canceled the trip. We decided that we would make the trip to K.C. in two weeks, the weekend of June 15th. School would be starting on July 9th. Looking for a place to live, just three weeks before the start of school was not in our original plans. It was also quite contrary to my basic plan-everything-ahead nature. The next morning, a package arrived in the mail from Cynthia Foster, a future classmate. The package contained home and apartment guides for the K.C. area. The following week my mother and my mother-in-law would both come to Chicago for a visit. I do not know how we ever arranged that. However, both of our moms were real estate agents. We told them the area we wanted to live in and the price range. They went through the home guides and started making phone calls to real estate agents in the K.C. area. They planned our home search and set up six homes for us to tour.

Our trip to K.C. on June 15th went smoothly. We looked at the six homes our mothers had set up with the realtor, but none really fit our needs. The real estate agent suggested we look at one more house. It had just come on the market the day before; it was not even in the multiple listings yet, but it did happen to be just what we wanted: three bedrooms, a fully finished basement, a very large backyard with a swing set (for Shavonne, who was three at the time), and it had a five-acre city park that backed up to the house. If we had gone on Memorial Day weekend, this house would not have been available and many of the places we had planned to go would probably have been closed for the holiday!

We decided to make a bid on the house, and that is when the real miracle occurred. The real estate agent asked how we planned to purchase the house. You know, the thought had never really crossed our minds. We had very good credit, and our house in Chicago was sure to sell very quickly, but neither one of us would be working (I would be going to school full time, and my wife would stay home and take care of our three-year-old daughter), so what bank would lend us money? The real estate agent just looked at us a little curiously, and then said we had better talk with his mortgage adviser. The mortgage adviser listened to our story in amusement and disbelief. Then he told us we really only had one option, and gave us a game plan on how to complete the deal. Now this man would gain nothing from the venture. The owners of the house also owned and were living in a house in Springfield, Missouri, which is a few hours south of K.C. They still held a mortgage on the house in K.C., but it was small, because they had owned the house for 28 years and it was just about paid for. The owners would need to hold the mortgage on the house, and we would have to make a down-payment large enough to pay off their mortgage with a little to spare, to give them incentive to deal. We would also have to agree that we would pay the remainder of the asking price of the house, once our house in Chicago sold. The mortgage adviser concluded by saying, "But, all of this is a little much to ask for; I will be praying for you."

Later, the owner of the house told me that, at first, she really did not like this idea at all, but she decided to think it over and pray about it, because we seemed like nice people. As she thought about it, her logic kept saying "no," and the people she spoke with advised against it, but something kept telling her to accept the offer. So, the next day she said, "Yes!"

On July 7th we signed the papers to close the deal on our new home, and moved in. On July 9th I started school. The house proved to be an ideal setting for my family. Since we were able to pay off the house from the profits of the sale of our house in Chicago, we were able to live rent-free for two years. The only needs we had to concern ourselves with were food, utilities and tuition.

Life is like floating, but we need to build our awareness of God's Sea of Life, because the Infinite One works in our lives in very mysterious ways, and through unexpected people and circumstances. You know that is true when both your mother and mother-in-law come to visit during the same week, and somehow everything worked together for good.

Well, you would think that after such a wonderful series of synchronistic manifestations, and all the magical things that had happened over those few years, that I would have completely figured out how this concept of trusting the *Infinite One* worked. Sadly to say, after I got all settled into our new home and began my studies at the Village, I fell back into my long-held habits of doubt, worry, and anxiety. I would look at my checkbook and wonder how I was going to make it through the next two years of ministerial school without working. Therefore, I relented, and did the logical thing; I looked for a variety of part-time jobs. Most of the time they were related in some way to my studies: working with the retreat department as a tour guide of the grounds; meeting guests at the airport and coordinating rides; being a helping hand at workshops and seminars; and the one I loved most, picking up guest speakers and presenters at the airport. These jobs helped to ease my doubt and anxiety, and provided enough income to meet our basic necessities.

At the end of the first year, I got sick and had to be rushed to the emergency room. After several frustrating hours, I was released with no diagnosis—perhaps it was an allergic reaction to some peanuts I ate, perhaps it was just nerves and anxiety. However, now I had a $1200 emergency room bill, and no money to pay it with; that is, if I wanted to pay my second year's tuition. I just looked at the bill and said aloud, "Okay, God, what am I going to do? Please tell me." Well, I did not hear an immediate response being shouted down from the heavens, but my wife Yvonne sensed my panic, called the hospital, and somehow got the bill reduced by about half. Then, two days later, I got a letter in the mail from the school. Immediately, I went into a panic mode and thought, *"My tuition is due. What I am going to do?"* Of course, it was the tuition statement, but there was another letter inside. I had been awarded a special scholarship for the many ways I had helped around the school, and the leadership example I had set. Not only was my tuition paid in full, but all of my required books were paid for as well. Wow!

Life is like floating, but we need to build our awareness of God's Sea of Life, because the Infinite One works in our life in very mysterious ways. We only need to relax and trust the Sea of Life to support us. There have been so many times that I have felt like Peter, sinking because I lacked the faith and trust; only to be rescued by Spirit, as it quietly whispers, "You of little faith, why do you doubt?"

Why did I doubt? In that moment, I made the commitment to myself that I would give up that old habit of doubt and anxiety. I certainly did not need it anymore. It was just a waste of my energy and made me sick. I was going to commit myself to learn to walk in faith, to step out on the Sea of Life and trust it to support me—in whatever I chose to do. If the financing did not come through to support my path, than I was not meant to do it. I knew God had not brought me this far to let me drown.

Therefore, I gave up all the little jobs I was doing here and there, except the ones I really liked, and began to do only things I would do if I were in a ministry. Suddenly, I began to get invitations to speak at various small churches around Kansas City and western Missouri. Often, when I would go to my mailbox, it would contain a check made out to me, sent from people I had never met and churches I had never been to, and always arriving just in time to pay off bills that had just come in the mail. Amazingly, I received more than $20,000 in gifts, tithes, and scholarship money during my second year in ministerial school. Now that is a very nice income, if you have no rent to pay and you are not working full time.

For me, ministerial school was a journey through a wilderness, filled with obstacles and challenges, a wilderness that taught me about the process of breaking through my fears—a process of learning to trust the sea of life to support me. This process of trusting and breaking through my fears made me feel as if I had walked off a cliff and was free falling, to suddenly be caught by the loving arms of Spirit. Certainly, financing ministerial school was an interesting proposition, not being able to work full time and still having to find a way to support my family. I learned to focus my attention on my relationship with God. I learned to trust the Infinite One as my source, and I was provided for very well. I cannot say I understand how the process works, but I have learned not to question it. I just trust, have faith, take the action I am guided to do, and Spirit does the rest.

To experience the goodness of life, we need only to let go of our doubts and worries, and open ourselves up to becoming aware of the synchronicity in our life, to how Spirit works and prompts us. Listen to Spirit's guidance. Take action according to the guidance you receive, watch for the results, and then, practice, practice, practice—allowing that sense of oneness to overtake you. The key is in trusting the sea of life; then you will feel that life is like floating on the breath and substance of God.

As I trust the sea of life to support me,
I realize that I am floating on the breath of the Infinite!

Resources for this Chapter

- The Holy Bible, New Revised Standard Version.

Lost On A Country Road

I am open and receptive to the inspiration of Spirit!

O Lord you have searched in me and know me.
You know when I sit down and when I rise up;
And you discern my thoughts ... you are acquainted with all my ways.
Even before a word is on my tongue, you know it completely ...
Where can I go from your Spirit?
If I ascend to Heaven you are there,
If I make my bed in She 'ol you are there.
If I take the wings of the morning and settle at the farthest limits
of the sea,
Even there your hand shall lead me ...
The 139th Psalm (verses 1-10)

The 139th Psalm indeed is a very powerful psalm. As I read the words, I can begin to feel and sense the very special relationship that King David of Israeli must have had with God. The 139th psalm, which is said to have been written by David, tells us that David knew God as an "Ever-Present Force" that surrounded and enfolded him and went wherever he went—often arriving at the destination before David did. David intuitively knew God, and he trusted the guidance he received from this

Ever-Present Force in his life. As David listened to the still, small voice of Spirit, which came to him in quiet moments, he learned that its guidance was never wrong. He developed a very strong faith, realizing that he was part of something that was much greater than himself.

As I read this psalm, I sense that David could see and feel this invisible force surrounding and enfolding him. David could see beyond the appearances of his physical reality; he grasps hold of the invisible matrix of life that is God. As a result of his ability to develop this gift, David had a very clear sense of direction for his life; consequently, he was able to lead the ancient Kingdom of Israel into its golden era. Would you not love to have that same intuitive ability—to be able see into and feel this ever-expanding field of life that we are immersed within and part of? Would you not love to be able discern your direction in life as well as David did? The truth is, you can too!

Speaking about direction, do you believe that you have a great sense of direction? Now truthfully, have you ever been lost? I am not talking a little lost. I mean really lost. Lost on a country road. Well, I think that I have a great sense of direction, and I rarely get lost; but when I do, I just pretend I am exploring!

I do know of at least one time that I was good and lost. A few years ago, my family and I were living in Kansas City and we decided to drive down to Orlando, Florida for vacation. It was a great trip. We went to Magic Kingdom, Epcot Center, Universal Studios, and Sea World. The trip was worth it, just to watch my then five year-old daughter's face light up every time she saw one of the Disney characters she knew. In fact, we spent the first two days standing in line to meet the different characters that she had been watching on television. She never did notice that these characters were all just regular people dressed in costumes.

However, the real adventure started on our drive back to Kansas City. We decided to take a different way home from the all-interstate one recommended by AAA. The route would take us through the northeast corner of Arkansas, where we could stop and visit with my wife's mother, who lives in a small rural town in the Ozark Mountains. Therefore, we charted our course and off we went.

When we arrived in Arkansas, we spotted on the map what appeared to be a short cut; that is, until the pavement ended and we were on a gravel road. The gravel soon disappeared and we were traveling down a bumpy dirt road about twenty miles per hour. We had traveled about fifteen miles off the main highway, and thought we should be almost to our destination when the dirt road made a wide sweeping turn and headed north. Over the ridge of the road, I spotted another smaller dirt road that continued off to the west; it looked seldom used and there was not a sign anywhere. In fact, there was not another soul in sight. I mean we were definitely lost out on a country road—no houses, no other cars, and I realized even if I wanted to ask for directions, there was no one around.

Which reminds me of what my wife always asks me, when we are in similar situations: "Do you know why Moses spent forty years wandering in the wilderness? He would not stop and ask for directions!" I am quite sure he would have said, "I am not lost; I'm just exploring." Well, I was beginning to feel a little bit like Moses.

Now, my intuition said to go straight, follow that road that looks like it is the road less traveled, keep heading west. *"But no!* I thought, *"I have been on this road for some time; it has got to be the right dirt road. It definitely looks like it is more traveled than that one that runs off into the woods. I better stick to the road that I know and have been traveling—after all, I do not want to get more lost."*

Right! Lost is lost and I am not quite sure if you can be "more lost," but I decided that I would rather stick with the lost I already knew, as opposed to choosing a new lost.

How many times in our lives, do we know that we are lost on the path we are currently traveling; and yet, we choose to continue down the same old, bumpy, uncomfortable path? At least it is familiar, and choosing a new path would mean we might have to give up what we have grown accustomed. Perhaps we stay on that old worn-out path because we are determined to prove this choice was the right one all along, or maybe we are afraid we will choose another lost path. We forget entirely about the possibility that a new choice might lead to the path that we have been searching for.

So, I continued northward on the same road I was traveling, although I knew I really needed to be going west. Do you know we did not pass a house or a car for miles? Finally, we came to another road that headed off to the west. Again, it looked like it just ran off into the woods, with no signs or markers. Only this one looked even more deserted. My intuition said a little bit louder, "Take the road west." However, I thought, *"I know this road; it may be rough, and bumpy, but it least it is familiar. The main road has just got to be up here a little bit further."* So, we continued heading north.

When we came to the third road that headed off to the west, I did not even slow down. By this time, my intuition was screaming. You know, the intuition, it is supposed to be that still, small voice that speaks to us from the center of our being, a quiet voice of guidance. Well, my intuition was shouting, "Turn around, go back, and take that road west!" But my consciousness mind said, "Oh no, I know this road ..." A few miles later, we saw a car traveling south, in the opposite direction. I did not think about it twice; I stopped them and asked for directions. Do you know what they told us? They said that the road we were traveling on would end in about a mile. When it did, we should turn left, head west, and in about half mile, we would come to the main road!

We had been driving down that bumpy, dusty dirt road for almost twenty miles, running parallel to the main highway, which was less than a mile away! Had I only listened to the guidance of my intuition, we would have found our way quickly and easily. As I drove down that very smooth highway, I passed each one of the other dirt roads I had chosen not to follow, and I thought about the course of my life. How easy it is for us to ignore the guidance of our intuition and simply follow the path in life that we have been traveling. The road may be rough, and our life may be filled with bumps and challenges, but at least it is familiar—at least we know what to expect.

However, if we follow the guidance of our intuition and trust the ways of *Spirit*, we will find that a new, smoother highway in life is just a short distance away. We merely need to make the choice to follow the path that *Spirit* has set out for before us. The road may take us into unknown terrain, and unexplored areas in our life, but just like King David, when we trust God and allow Spirit to take charge, the way will be made easy. Oh, how easy that may sound like it is to do, and yet ... oh how hard. Why? Because we always want to do it our way; it may be tough, but at least it is familiar.

Then there are those who ask, "How can I tell the difference between the voice of the intuition from the other thoughts and messages that I receive from other sources? How can I trust it?" The book of Isaiah, chapter 41, offers these words from Spirit: "Listen to me in silence, let the people renew their strength, let them approach; then let them speak; let us together draw near for spiritual discernment."

Yes, listen for the Voice of Spirit in the silence; it is here we regain our strength, and then speak the desire of our heart. As we do, we merge with Spirit and are guided to the answers we seek. Indeed, prayer is the master key in life, the key that unlocks the doorway to the intuition.

What is the intuition? The intuition is a natural "knowing capacity" in each of us, a gift of Spirit, a feeling of sure knowing that comes in spite of appearances. Many have called the intuition the wisdom of the heart. When we trust Spirit and look to It for understanding, a certain confidence in the realm of invisible good begins to develop.[21] This exercising of our faith helps to awaken a sixth sense within us. Through this power of intuition, we have direct access to all knowledge and all the wisdom in this realm of ever-expanding spiritual potential.

Indeed, this intuitive knowing is the voice of Spirit calling. It is our source of a deeper understanding of the way Spirit expresses in the world. This "knowing" capacity transcends intellectual knowledge, or any knowledge that is gained through the filters of our perceptions. It is most often heard as a still, small voice that speaks from the depths of our being.

Yes, prayer is the "narrow way" that leads to the purest expression of the intuition, but not the repetitious verbal prayers that many of us learned as kids, and practice as adults. That type of prayer will not lead us to a place in consciousness where we can hear this still, small voice. This practice of verbalizing our prayers in public is just the opposite of the way Jesus instructed us to pray. He said, "Go into your inner room and shut the door and pray to your Father, who hears in secret, and there He will recompense thee" (Matthew 6:6 NRSV)."

Pray for guidance and direction in the silence of meditation, and then search for the quiet space between your thoughts. We need to practice listening and waiting in the stillness, in the quite spaces, where the presence of Spirit can be felt. Then watch during the activity of the day for answers

---

21 *The Revealing Word*, by Charles Fillmore, published by Unity Books, Unity Village Missouri

to come, for the answers we seek surely will come. The only question that remains is: "Will we be ready for the answers and know when they have arrived?"

In other words, we need to become more conscious of life, and study the different thoughts that go through our mind. Watch the thoughts as they pass by, and listen in the space *between* our thoughts. Soon, we will become aware of the flow, the rhythm, and the synchronicity within our life. For me, the guidance I receive from my intuition is normally calm and peaceful; it is a sense of pure knowing that I have. However, it can be different for others.

When we seek God and become aware of our oneness with God, as Jesus did, as King David did, we begin to experience this overwhelming sense of peace and harmony in all circumstance. When we dwell in the shelter of the Most High in a regular pattern of prayer and meditation, we become open and receptive to the flow of Spirit. We realize that the angels of the Most High will lead us to the right people and the right circumstance. The right doors open at the right time. When we become aware of the support of God and His abundant, loving universe, we feel like we are floating on an ocean of God's support. It is through prayer and this process of active listening, that we learn to trust the guidance we receive from our intuition.

However, I have found that many of us do our prayer work, and we try our hand at meditation, yet deep down we do not really believe in the power of the mental work that we are doing. We do not fully believe that we can draw forth a manifestation from the realm of substance into our physical world. Therefore, when our answer lies right before our eyes, we do not recognize it. We do not even consider the possibility, and yet, this is the primary way we learn to differentiate the "voice" of the Holy Spirit from our other thoughts and promptings.

When we have one of the "ah ha" experiences in life, we can finally see how the pieces we have been struggling with all fit together. Did we do it? NO! The Infinite One, God's Spirit, helped us to be aware of it. Just like when I was lost on that country road. Our life experience, when combined with our inner knowing about an event, will provide us valuable insights in how to understand the way our intuition and our other thoughts communicate to us. However, we must be willing to listen and be open to the possibilities!

The trouble is when we fail to listen to our inner knowing about the experiences in our life, we will keep re-living the experiences over and over again, falling deeper and deeper into the darkness. It is like traveling down the same bumpy, uncomfortable dirt road over and over again, until we finally decide to make the proper turn. Sooner or later we will get the message. Once we begin to understand the way Spirit communicates to us, we can hear the voice of our intuition clearly, and we begin to see God's message everywhere. Like traveling down a road over and over again, and then suddenly you notice something you have never seen before; it might be a huge billboard that grabs your attention, only it has always been there. You have been distracted with other things you thought were more important. So listen to your feelings, and your highest thought, search the spaces between your thoughts, and watch your experiences. Learn to trust the inner voice, that quiet voice of sure knowing, which whispers to you from beyond the stillness.

As I drove down that highway in Arkansas, I realized a valuable lesson. When I pray and ask for guidance in my life, I now ask myself, "Am I really open and receptive to the guidance I seek, even if it looks very different than I may suppose." We all have free will to choose. We can choose to stay lost on an old, bumpy road in our life that simply has become familiar, or we can trust Spirit to be in charge and follow the direction of "The Still, Small Voice." Know that the invisible source of life is guiding you to the right road, which leads to an experience of God's Kingdom of good.

I am open and receptive to the inspiration of Spirit!

Resources for this Chapter

- The Revealing Word, Charles Fillmore, Unity Books, Unity Village Missouri

- Dynamics For Living, Charles Fillmore, Unity Books, Unity Village Missouri

- Teach Us To Pray, Charles Fillmore, Unity Books, Unity Village Missouri

- The Holy Bible, New Revised Standard and King James Versions

Hold the Oregano Please!

I still myself in the moment and call forth the wisdom of the Indwelling Spirit,
So that I can see past appearances to the heart of every matter

Have you ever had an experience that made you want to laugh and cry at the same time? An event that filled you with both anger and compassion, and left you mired in thought, saying to yourself, "How could I have handled this differently? There must have been another way!"

A number of years ago—when I was living in Columbus, Ohio—Yvonne, Shavonne and I decided to get away from it all by driving out to one of the state parks in southwestern Ohio. On our way, we stopped in a small town near the park to get lunch. The two main restaurants had long waits. We were really hungry, so waiting was not an option. Thinking we might get something quickly, we chose to go to Subway. When we entered the store, all the seats were full and there was a short line at the counter. We got into the line and waited while the counter girl worked with the customers in front of us. I silently wondered whether, or not, we would be able to find a table once we had our food.

Finally, it was our turn. Yvonne and Shavonne both ordered sandwiches, while I choose a salad. The sandwiches were quickly made and when she began to make my salad, she asked if I would like oregano, to which I answered, "Yes, I love it."

As she began to shake the oregano, I heard someone begin to yell. It was a loud, booming voice that was filled with anger and rage, "Why haven't you got that boy's paycheck yet? Why are you making him wait like this?" As he yelled, the counter girl continued to shake the oregano. She looked up and responded, "I've been busy." I naturally looked over my shoulder, to see who this madman was, and I could not believe my eyes! It was a policeman!

He then demanded, "When you finish with this customer, I want you to stop taking customers and get his paycheck. I don't care if you have to lock the door, but you are not going to take any more customers."

Although during his tirade, the few customers who would come in the door turned around and left, and the ones who were already seated were jumping up and scurrying out the door. Well, I guess I didn't have to worry about there being any empty tables. The policeman continued to rant and rave at the lady behind the counter. He was shaking his finger in her face, as if scolding a child. She was visibly shaking, and yes, she was still holding and shaking that oregano container over my salad.

Finally, she was able to break into his tirade. As she did, she set down the jar of oregano, and responded, "I don't know what you want me to do! I do not know where the check is. I have called the store's owner, but his line was busy. When I am done with this customer, I will call him again."

The policeman started screaming at the lady again. He was very abrasive, loud, and demanding. The veins in his neck were popping out and I could feel his rage and anger exploding into the atmosphere. It was really making me uncomfortable; I had seen this type of anger before, and I knew from past experiences not to say anything at all. I stopped looking at him and just stared at my salad that was sitting on the other side of the counter. I thought, *"I wish he would stop yelling at her so she could finish my salad and I could leave."* As I did, I heard a very familiar voice speaking my very thoughts, out loud. It was my wife, Yvonne. She said, "Excuse me! Would you just leave her alone and let her finish making our order, so we can pay for it and leave? Then you can finish this debate."

The officer now turned and took two steps towards my wife, and directed his anger towards her. He began shaking his finger at my wife and yelled, "You be quiet or I'll arrest you!"

In disbelief, Yvonne replied, "Arrest me? You're going to arrest me?"

The officer of the peace yelled back, "That's right, I can and will arrest you for-for-" he stammered, trying to find justification for the threat, "-for obstruction! 'Cause you're interfering with official police business!" I thought the only thing she was obstructing was his anger.

When I looked at my wife, she had one of *those* looks on her face. You know the kind of look I am talking about. The kind that says, "I was raised on the streets of Chicago; I've seen far more intimidating people than you, some Barney Fife country bumpkin. Look out, because I am going to teach you a lesson." I could see it coming: her throwing her arms out in front of him and saying, "I dare you! Arrest me! Go ahead, I dare you!" I just looked at her and thought, *"Dear God, don't let her do it."* God must have intervened, because Yvonne paused for a moment, and thought again and then backed off.

The policeman turned his attention back to the counter person and continued his barrage. The woman behind the counter finally cried out, "All right already! I will stop what I am doing and call the owner." Then she left, leaving my salad sitting on the other side of the counter just beyond my reach—and I was so hungry.

Finally, another woman appeared out of nowhere to finish our order. As she picked up the container on the counter, I said, "Hold the oregano, please. I have had quite enough." My wife was now very angry and was trying desperately to restrain herself from saying anything further, knowing she would probably be arrested if she said what was on her mind. I thought, so much for getting something quick to eat. We paid for our meals and went to sit at one of the many empty tables.

A few minutes later, I watched the young man leave, jubilantly, with his check, while I tried to explain what had just happened to my then seven-year-old daughter. However, the only thing I could remember was something I had heard my parents say many times: "Two wrongs don't make a right." Yes, it was wrong for the store to withhold the young man's check, but the actions of the policeman were also wrong, and were, as we later found out, far beyond that policeman's jurisdiction.

My wife and I were troubled by the events and struggled for answers. I thought, *"How could we have acted differently? How could we have been an instrument of God's peace and love in the midst of turmoil? Was there something we could have done or said that would have diffused the anger being expressed?*

Why did I once again find myself in the midst of such an anger-filled situation? How could we have just randomly walked into a restaurant, in a small country town, miles from our home, and find ourselves enmeshed in controversy?" I knew I had something to learn, and this was an opportunity to do so.

Yvonne felt we really needed to do something about what had transpired, and I agreed, so we spent the next two hours at the police station, filing a complaint with the chief of police. What a great way to "get away from it all!" As I sat in the police station, I thought about that afternoon, and realized that the policeman had a perfect right to his anger, although it was clearly exaggerated and inappropriately expressed. To burst into a place of business and disrupt the operations is not acceptable. To vent your anger on others is not acceptable. Perhaps the boy's situation provoked memories of a bad experience the policeman once had, and he saw an opportunity to set things straight. Perhaps he witnessed the activity through the filter of his personal beliefs, a filter that had been clouded by the darkness of his work. Perhaps he reacted, not according to the situation, but from the pain he had buried in his subconscious.

Remember, we are seldom upset for the reasons we think. Often when we take a closer look at our reaction, we find our reaction is not the result of the activities of the present moment, but of things, of memories, of experiences we have pushed down into the subconscious. There these memories are compressed, repressed and coiled to wait for the perfect opportunity to explode on some unsuspecting person. This tints everything we see, and poisons us from the inside out. When I spoke to the police chief, he informed me that the officer denied yelling at the lady behind the counter, and was not even aware that he'd expressed any anger at all. It is a human tendency: when we get caught in reliving our past we are often unaware of the extent of our emotional outburst. The policeman did not realize that his behavior had emptied out an entire restaurant in just a few minutes.

It was obvious, at least to me, that this man was suppressing years of hurt and pain, and was a time bomb waiting to explode. His expression of anger was a call for help—it was a call for love. I suggested to the chief that, instead of taking the matter to court, or to a board for review, when he had finished gathering information, he recommend that the policeman get some meaningful counseling, or they might find themselves with a much bigger problem. The police chief smiled, nodded, and then said, "Yes, that would probably be a very good thing to do. This particular officer has had a very rough time over the past few months."

Needless to say, our trip was dominated by the disturbance. I thought to myself, *"How could I have responded differently? There must have been another way!"* When we arrived home, Yvonne sat down to pray and then reached over and picked up a book. It happened to be *Myrtle Fillmore's Healing Letters*. She opened it at random, as she often does when searching for answers, and then began to read.

66

"Instead of thinking of the people whom you have believed to be evil, and an undesirable influence, begin to think of the goodness of God's life within all of God's children. Think of God as everywhere present light, love, peace, and life. Think of all men, all women, all children as ever abiding in God's presence and expressing God's qualities. As you do this, you will touch the reality of individuals, you will touch the fabric of their being, and you will invite only the best from them. Spirit will respond as you expect it to, for the Spirit of God is in each and every person. Some persons have not yet awakened to this realization. However, as you declare the Truth for them, expect to have it express through them towards you, and you will receive only loving and considerate treatment from them. The best way to see your brother is to see them spiritually illumined. See the indwelling Christ within them."[22]

99

Although this can be a difficult thing to remember when you are caught up in turbulence, there is a place of strength and love and peace within you—a touchstone so to speak, that can be activated at any time. If you can still your mind in the heat of the moment, you can go to that place and call up its strength and guidance and it will guide your words and actions. You will be able to listen with love and understanding and you will be able to recognize the "call for love," and get to the heart of the matter. When we meet anger with resistance and more anger, we provoke an escalation of the other person's anger and we become caught

---

22 *Myrtle Fillmore's Healing Letters*, Myrtle Fillmore, Unity Books, Unity Village, MO

in the cycle of hate that grows out of control. Whenever we find anger and hatred being expressed, love, compassion, and understanding are the only answer.

Do you have challenging individuals in your life? As you sit in times of quiet prayer and meditation, visualize those individuals being immersed in the love, light, and life of God. See only the best for them, see the Christ awakening and emerging from their being. Visualize them spiritually illumined. See the indwelling Christ within them. Then, when you look into their eyes, you will touch the fabric of their being, and you will be transformed. Your life will never be the same. Look past appearances, seeing to the heart of the matter. You might even remember to say, "Hold the oregano, please."

I still myself in the moment and calling forth the wisdom of in the Indwelling Spirit

I see past appearances to the heart of every matter

Resources for this chapter:

- A Course In Miracles, Inner Peace Foundation, Tiburon, CA

- What You Can Feel You Can Heal, A Guide for Enriching Relationships, John Gray, Ph.D., Heart Publications, Mill Valley CA

- Myrtle Fillmore's Healing Letters, Myrtle Fillmore, Unity Books, Unity Village, MO

Deeper Things

As I open my heart and mind to Spirit, I am guided to the deeper things of life

On my last trip to Unity Village, I went for a walk one morning, just to clear my mind and to find some peace from a night filled with storms and pouring rain. The air was clean, pure, and crisp and felt so good after the night of showers. I walked into the nearby woods, passing an outdoor chapel constructed to fit its natural surrounds. How perfect! I enjoyed the beauty of the morning, the warmth of the sun and the songs of the birds. As I walked along a rain-soaked path, mud and water filled my shoes, but something called me deeper.

Walking deeper into the woods, the path grew smaller and narrower as it meandered through the rain-soaked trees. I remembered a tale of a special place, a unique and solitary place. Not sure of where I was headed, I spotted what looked like a stone pathway, although it was difficult to tell because the stones were so worn and laid so unevenly. However, I followed them deeper, and deeper still, into the woods.

Suddenly, I could hear the sound of water running, a stream flowing somewhere just beyond my sight. I ducked under a branch, took a few more steps, and then there it was: a natural bridge—a cave that was open at both ends with the stream flowing through it. How beautiful! How peaceful and serene was this unseen place, protected and surrounded by the woods so that only explorers of deeper things would ever find it.

The beauty of the rock, the sound of the water, the darkness of the cave, and the light at the other end all invited me in. I entered the cave and walked from rock to rock across the stream, to stay above the water, but I became lost in a flow of thought that swept me away. Deeper and deeper still the urge was guiding me, and then I spotted an opening that led straight up and to the light. Looking up through the hole in the rocks, I could see blue skies, framed by the trees and the sandstone. Yet, I realized my journey was still not complete. The cave continued on, I could see the opening at the other end very clearly, as the water and the light streamed into the darkness of my surroundings. I stayed for a while, enjoying the beauty of the moment, reflecting on deeper things: the comfort of the cave, as dark and ominous as it appeared to be; the beauty of the light as it filtered in from the right and the left and from above. The light beckoned and urged me to return, but the comfort of this dwelling place was somehow so familiar and secure, from things above and far beyond, that it caused me to linger on and on.

At long last, I heard a clap of thunder and I knew the storms were going to return. So I hurried back to my cottage along the rocky, rain-soaked path, through the woods to more familiar things, making it through the door of the temporary residence just before the fresh new rains came pouring down.

As I sat in my room, dry and safe, I must admit part of me stayed behind to contemplate the deeper things. In that cave there was a point where the light came pouring in to dissolve the darkness. I was struck by the metaphor of life that this natural bridge presented. The light dispelled the darkness and urged me to return to the life that was teeming in the woods all about that cave. Yet, subconsciously, or perhaps consciously, the cave and its darkness felt comfortable and secure. Even though it seemed very odd, I could feel the *living waters of the Most High* flowing all about me. Yes, even there in the darkness, the *living waters* flowed.

My mind raced and searched to understand this darkness that the human side of me found to be so comforting and secure, so compelling and intriguing that it beckons to me even now as I type these words. There is a part of humankind that treasures the confined spaces of life; whether it is cave, a familiar living quarter, a memory, a state of mind, or a particular belief system. There is a certain comfort, a feeling of safety and well being, that comes from being in a space that is well known to us, or at least one where we can see and sense everything going on around us, even if it is in the darkness.

How often do we remain in the darkness and despair of our own life because it feels comfortable? I might be hurting and angry, filled with despair, but at least it is familiar and I know what to expect. How often do we remain tucked in bed, or stay at home, even though there might be many fun or enlightening or enriching things we could do, simply because we prefer the comfort and solitude of familiar surroundings? Something in our subconscious mind stirs, "If I go out there, into the light of the world, out there into the unknown, who knows what will happen?" Although the *light of the divine* filters into our darkness and beckons us to return to the fullness of life, we resist, preferring a darkness that we know.

The natural bridge reminded me of a story about a man who had been raised in a single room since childhood. Never having been out of the room, he learned from the few picture-less books he had that nothing but devastation existed outside his walls, and that he was alone. He lived on meager meals that appeared mysteriously through a small portal. He accepted his life, based on the facts of his reality, which was one of limitation and darkness. Meanwhile, he lived in the basement of a mansion of a huge estate that had every conceivable luxury and convenience.[23] In the same way, the woods surroundings that natural bridge provided the basis for every kind of life, while just fifteen to twenty feet below these woods teaming with life lay an underground shelter, undetected by mortal senses—a place of security, and a degree of comfort and relative peace. Although the light dispersed its darkness, you could not see into the cave beyond its borders, nor could you, when you were in that cave, see or feel the life present in the woods beyond its limits.

Likewise, most of humankind has taken up residence in one small room of the mansion called life. We have created walls in our minds that prevent us from seeing beyond our circumstances, or the framework of our individual belief systems. We cling to various limiting beliefs and restricting perceptions, holding to their illusions despite how illogical they might be, or how much pain they might create.

---

23 *Soul Power* Ernest Wilson, Unity Books, Unity Village, MO

Indeed, there are people today, some very prominent people, who are like that man living in the basement, refusing to go upstairs, declaring that because the upper rooms did not come down to him, they were not there and did not exist. This truly is the source of most of the problems we face, the inability and unwillingness to move beyond what we know and believe to be true. Even in "New Thought Circles," despite how open and receptive to new extensive concepts we claim to be, there are times when we have simply moved from one room to another. Perhaps it is a larger room. Perhaps we have even made it to the first floor of that mansion, but rarely do we make it outside into the gardens or to the woods beyond, where true life is experienced.

We have learned to wear our different masks, which hide and suppress our true selves so well that we have forgotten who we truly are; we have forgotten that we are beings of light and energy, whose souls' purpose is to return to the oneness of the spectrum of light and life. We need to step out of the caves and the darkness that our mortal minds have created, and into the light of our true reality.

I hear these very thoughts being echoed in Jesus' words when he said, "In my Father's House there are many dwelling places; if it were not so I would not have told you that I go to prepare a place for you. If I go and prepare a place for you, I will come again and will take you where I AM" (John 14:2 – 4). Although these words are often used during funeral services in reference to some afterlife experience, or by fundamentalist ministers as they preach about the end of times they say are foretold in *The Book of Revelation*, I believe they referred to a different reality; a reality that has always existed, right here. There are a multitude of different dwelling places for us to reside. Some are easily seen in this reality—like that cave or our own rooms in our homes—and other dwelling places are hiding in our minds, and present in our belief systems. While still other parts of our Father's house remain just beyond our sight in the realm of the unseen and the invisible.

A good example of this is our body. When we look down at it, it appears to be solid enough, but underneath the layers of skin are cells, bones, blood, nerves, organs, and just a whole bunch of stuff that cannot be seen by our eyes. In fact, quantum physicists now speculate that our bodies are 99.9% energy. When scientists looked at the cells of the human body, they found that they were composed of tiny molecules—clusters of atoms. When they looked inside the atom, which they once thought was the tiniest particle of solid matter, all they found was a field of energy, which had specks of small matter called electrons, neutrons, and protons. When they were finally able to look inside the electrons, neutrons, and protons, all they found was a field of energy, which had specks of still smaller matter floating around in it. Indeed, we are energy beings!

Now, I know that some mornings it certainly does not feel that way, as we lie in bed wondering, "When will I ever find the energy to get up?" Nevertheless, the energy is there. Why? Because we are energy beings! We just need to reach out with our awareness and channel our energy in a direction that will get us up and going.

Other "dwelling places" exist just beyond our sight in the realm of the invisible, just a few feet away. Call them dimensions, or realities, or whatever, but sometimes you can sense and feel them; sometimes you will catch a figure passing through the corner of your eye, was it a Spirit or an angel? Sometimes you may have what people have described as a mystical experience, when one of those other realities begins to blend into ours. It is as if we have somehow stepped out this physical reality and into another as our world slows down. I have had several such experiences.

One of them happened while I was at work, if you can believe that, while managing a hectic courier office. There were twenty people in the room. When I paused for a moment, time and space seemed to melt away as I felt this sense of oneness take over the room. While everyone else was focused on their roles, their voices blended together and the barriers and boundaries that normally separated us dissolved; the atoms of our being filled the room and floated there; and I felt this *Life-Force* permeating the room. Somehow, in this very busy courier office, I could hear both ends of all the telephone and two-way radio conversations. Although I had no phone, no radio headset, and really no way to do so, I could hear the caller on the other side of all the lines. I knew the answers to questions I was about to be asked before they were asked, and I gave my responses spontaneously, before the staff opened their mouths with their questions. As I did this time and time again, my staff's mouths would drop open, their heads would tilt to the side in utter amazement, and then they would say, "How did you know I was going to ask that?" It was maybe ten or fifteen minutes before I drifted out of the experience and was left with an overwhelming sense of awe.

A divine matrix of life surrounds, enfolds, and connects us with all of life, but we need to stretch our awareness of its presence if we are to evolve beyond our current dwelling place and reach our true potential. The field of life is not simply what can be seen and felt through our physical senses; it is an ocean of energy. Its invisible vibration creates and gives expression to a myriad of forms, whether seen or unseen. As we seek to widen our world by opening all our senses, both physical and spiritual, we begin to understand the deeper things of life and come to know a much larger reality.

Jesus had a much larger vision for humanity than simply following the Ten Commandments and basic moral teachings. He challenged us to step out of our caves when he said, "You are the light of the world … let your light shine before others." (Matthew 5:14). Jesus used this analogy of the inner light in a variety of ways and continually urged his disciples, and each of us, to step into a new reality. In the light of current discoveries, that we are 99.9% energy and that as energy moves it produces different levels, or bands of light, this statement made by Jesus takes on a whole new dimension, spiritually and scientifically.

Think about it! You are not your body; you were designed to be something much greater. What would it be like if we truly realized that we were created in the image and likeness of God and expressed it? God is Spirit, the breath and energy of life, moving energy and light. All that we see in the universe is God, Spirit—energy and light—being projected into visible forms. This is the truth of who we are. God as infinite life, love, wisdom, and abundance lies within every human being and is waiting to be called forth. The keys to the ever-expanding Kingdom of good are within our grasp! Is that not what Jesus repeated over and over again? "The time is now, the Kingdom of Heaven is at hand, turn to it and believe." (Mark 1:15).

Jesus tried to tell us that we have access to the *creative force of life*; we only need to seek its light and energy by removing the barriers that are blocking its expression in us.

In that cave, there was a point where the light came pouring in to dissolve the darkness. I could feel the promptings of the light urging me to return to the life that was teeming in the woods above, but I resisted. So often the caves of our mind, and its darkness, provide a certain level of comfort and a feeling of safety; at least it is familiar and we know what to expect. Even though we can feel and sense the *living waters* of the divine, this is not where we are meant to reside. We need to step out of the caves and the darkness that our mortal mind has created and into the light, to explore the deeper things of our true reality. As our minds open to this larger, more expansive image of Spirit presence, we will begin to feel the light and energy of the divine flowing through us, we will know that we are, indeed, just as Jesus said: "The light of the world!" You are the light of the world; so let your light shine.

As I open my heart and mind to Spirit, I am guided to the deeper things of life!

Reference for this Chapter

- <u>Soul Power</u>, Ernest Wilson, Unity Books, Unity Village, MO

- <u>The Holy Bible</u>, New Revised Standard Version

- <u>What the Bleep Do We Know</u>? The movie, Twentieth Century Fox Entertainment.

The Kingdom of Heaven Is Like An Onion

I am open to the fullness of life!

The Kingdom of Heaven is like an onion! Do you not love this statement? If you do not, you probably do not like onions! You should know, as someone who worked in the food industry for more than twenty years, I put onions in just about everything I fix. Sometimes they are very apparent and sometimes they are very well hidden in the blend of other ingredients. Onions seem to add a unique flavor and richness to everything. Yes indeed, I have found that the Kingdom of Heaven is like an onion.

No, this is not something Jesus said; although I often think it is similar to one of his teachings. Jesus was a carpenter, and I am a cook. Jesus explained this particular concept in relation to a house, which he shared with the disciples on the night of his last supper. The statement is recorded in the Gospel of John 14:1 – 4. Here Jesus said, "In my Father's house there are many mansions. If it were not so, would I have told you that I go to prepare a place for you? And if I go and prepare a place for you, I will come again and will take you to myself, so that where I am, there you may be also. And you know the way to the place where I am going."

What exactly did Jesus mean by this very cryptic message? Why did he not say exactly what he meant? Many groups in modern day Christianity teach that Jesus was speaking of some type of afterlife; that Heaven, being our Father's house, had many different levels and realities. Then one day, perhaps on the day of our passing from this physical plane,

Jesus would return to escort those who were deserving to this place called heaven, which he had made ready. This is indeed a very comforting and reassuring thought. I could definitely buy this understanding.

Other groups insist that this will only happen at the time of the second coming, the day they believe Jesus will return, to take a selected few into Heaven to be with him, while the rest of humanity is left behind—an event they believe to be prophesied in the Book of Revelations. But a literal interpretation of this literature, which has been termed apocalyptic (a Greek word meaning "to reveal" or "to unveil," and suggests something had been hidden within its text that was highly symbolic), would seem to defy logic.[24] [25] It is also an idea that seems to defy the heart and soul of Jesus' teachings, which focused on love, forgiveness, and non-judgment.

According to the Gospel records, Jesus talked often about this place he called "Heaven." He described it as an ever-present reality, as something that was within our grasp, an ever-expanding creative potential that was here now. So, merely describing heaven—our Father's house, a place that has many mansions—simply as an afterlife experience we might possibly get to go to one day (after we leave this physical realm) seems to fall short of Jesus' promise, and what I believe to be his intended meaning. Consider these words spoken by Jesus, which are recorded in the Gospel of Luke: "The Kingdom of God is not coming with things that can be observed; nor will they say, 'Look, here it is!' or 'There it is!' For, in fact, the Kingdom of God is in the midst of you." (Luke 17:21 – 20)

Heaven is not simply an afterlife experience; it is here now, in the midst of you right now! Jesus continually taught us about this good news, saying all we had to do was turn to it and believe.

But, you say, "Why can I not see it or sense it or feel it?" Well, that is because the Kingdom of Heaven is like an onion. Like our Father's house, an onion has many different layers and realities, or should I say dwelling places. What does this mean?

Many years ago, when I worked in the restaurant industry, one of my jobs was as the food prep manager for a very successful restaurant

---

24 The Interpreter's One-Volume Commentary on the Bible, Abingdon Press, Nashville, Tennessee pg 1106

25 Revelation the Road to Overcoming, Charles Neal, Unity Books, Unity Village Missouri

in the Washington, D.C. area. Each day we would have to slice and dice fifty to a hundred pounds of onions. That is a lot of onions! All of these onions had to be cut by hand. Anyone who has tried to slice onions in a food processor quickly finds they have a juicy mess on their hands. After slicing and dicing hundreds of pounds of onions by hand, over several months, you might say I have a very special relationship with onions.

Have you ever looked at an onion closely? When most people first look at an onion, they see flaky skins and rough root ends. When you clear away the outer layer and cut the edges, you find a tough outer layer that has been hardened by its exposure to the dirt and the air—by the physical elements of its life. When you peel away this layer, you find a softer interior layer, and then another and another until you reach the core—the heart of the onion, which is soft and tender and, believe it or not, has a sweet and rich flavor.

If the onion has a consciousness (and I do not totally dismiss the idea), it would be a good bet that one layer would not know that the other layers existed, even though it is lying right there next to another layer just fractions of millimeters away. Each layer is whole and complete, just as it is. Each layer has it own membrane, flavor and shape.

Now that you know more about an onion than you probably ever wanted to know, how is the Kingdom of Heaven like an onion? How is it like our Father's house that has many mansions? Michael Beckwith, probably the most successful "new thought" minister of our time, teaches that there are four stages in our spiritual evolution. I believe that this is a good starting place to begin the discussion. Whether or not, there are exactly four is open for debate, but one thing is sure is that there are at least four and maybe more different layers to our spiritual evolution. Likewise, our awareness of the Kingdom of Heaven is experienced in different layers, just like an onion.

What exactly am I saying? I believe we are immersed within an ocean of God life; it surrounds and enfolds us. Someone once asked me, "Does God exist?" I answered them "No, God does not exist—God "IS" existence—a Force that flows and moves through all of creation, an energy field, a divine wisdom and life that permeates all things."

Remember, the only way Jesus ever described God was *as* Spirit (John 4:24). Jesus did not say that God was *a* Spirit, he said, "God *is* Spirit, and those who worship God must worship God in Spirit and truth." God *is* Spirit, a divine matrix of energy and life, in whom, as Paul said, "we live and move and have our being" (Acts 17:28).

The only way we can come into an awareness of this infinite force is through the level of our own awareness—through the "layer" of what we have experienced in life and been taught by others, as children and adults. We learn about God, the Infinite One, the Creator or whatever you call that divine force, through our experiences and how we personally relate to life. This layer, often called our belief system, only changes and moves when life forces us to change or stretch beyond our current level of awareness. We simply do not know any other layer exist, because it exists outside of our current layer/level of awareness.

This is perhaps the single biggest reason why so many different religions and spiritual paths exist. We all need to find our path to God, our own way to relate to the infinite. Although we often join together on one path—on one of layer awareness—there are infinite ways/journeys/layers for us to experience the way the divine moves in us. My experience of the infinite is probably not the same as yours. Jesus' experience and beliefs about God, *the Father within*, were different than Paul's ideas of *Christ*, and different than Isaiah's belief in the *"anointing of Spirit."* Each described this same divine force in different ways.

Indeed the Kingdom of Heaven can be compared to an onion. When you first look at an onion, you see the outside layer, the flaky outer part that is exposed to the physical elements of dirt and air. Spiritually and metaphysically, you would say this represents that part of us that is more worldly and grounded in the physical illusion of this reality. Just as the outer skin of the onion is exposed to the darkness of the earth for most of its existence, those who experience the Infinite One from this layer/level of awareness are filled by a certain darkness about life. They live in the darkness of their mind, and know little about the true light and life of Spirit. This is why Jesus said, "No one after lighting a lamp puts it under the bushel basket, but on the lamp stand, and it gives light to all in the house. In the same way, let your light shine before others" (Matthew 5:15).

Many people walk in the darkness and they do not even know it. They might attend church, but they have never been taught that this *light* is within them. It is from this layer of their awareness that they see the world and experience the infinite as if it exists somewhere out there, outside of them selves. They walk in a cloud wherever they go and long for something, something that simply cannot be filled by outer things, although this is exactly how they seek to fill the void that exists in them.

If you walk into a store, you can see the actions of some parents managing their kids in violent ways. Often, these parents have a vacant or lost look. Perhaps you know someone like this. They are everywhere. Indeed, they seem like the flaky outer layer of awareness, which is very delicate, and falls apart if touched. They spend much of their attention on the outer problems. Focusing on what they believe they need and want and how others are responsible for what they are experiencing. They think, *"If only I had this that ..."* or *"If so and so would stop trying to destroy my happiness, life would be better."* Michael Beckwith describes this first layer as those who see life just happening to them; that they are victims of life.

The next layer on the onion is a tough outer layer; it is good for soup stock but not much else. This layer represents an awareness that has been hardened by life. These individuals have made progress, because they are holding their lives together, but they really do not have any idea of where they are headed. They have seen far too much darkness in life, living close to the physical illusions of life, and in fear of the things that could happen. They believe they have little control over their life and see themselves at the hands of an unmerciful and fickle God, who for some reason has decided to punish them. Their motto is, "Hold onto all you can before it slips away."

As you peel away each layer of the onion, you realize that as you approach the center, each layer becomes softer and softer. Likewise, the deeper and deeper you seek to take your relationship with the Infinite One, your relationship becomes more tender, fuller and sweeter, although the layers remains quite separate. Have you ever noticed that sometimes you can talk to a person and they seem to be so in-tune with you, that they see life from the same perspective? Then, you talk to someone else who seems to be living in a completely different time zone or a different reality altogether. Well, they are! They are living in a different layer of awareness.

Once you have removed all the outer layers of the onion, you come to the core—its heart. Likewise, on our spiritual journey into the Kingdom of Heaven, we have different layers of awareness to remove: a flaky skin; a hard, chewy outer layer; and layers of life issues and beliefs that have kept us from experiencing what all of us desire the most to know: God. We want to be able to live fully in an awareness of light and life of the divine. What is this like? Jesus said, "The Father and I are one" (John 10:30). "As the Father is in me, so *I AM* in you (John 17:21)." Buddha said, "I am awake, I am aware." The great *I AM*, is God. The *I AM* is a point, a place in our awareness where the Divine has cleared away all the darkness, all boundaries, all barriers, and we feel the oneness of true life. It is a place *in our awareness* that *feels* like a flow of energy, a connectedness, and helps us to feel as if we are indeed the light of the world.

This concept is really hard to explain because so few people in our day and age are willing to talk about it. Although, I would venture to say that ministers of all denominations have experienced it. When we reach our spiritual core, there is a dropping away of personal boundaries and an inflow of energy and life, which produces a feeling of oneness and intuitive knowing. Sometimes this peak experience is confused with the emotions of love for a particular individual. However, it is much more than that and has nothing to do with the individual standing before us.

Musicians will, at times, find themselves so in tune with the energy of the music that every thing else drops away and they feel "the Spirit;" that is to say they feel the Spirit of the infinite flowing through them. There is an often-repeated phrase in the Bible that describes this experience: *"the Spirit of the Lord came upon them."* It is like sticking your finger in a spiritual light socket, and you are charged with spiritualized energy and aliveness. There is nothing like it. Any attempt to explain it is really not possible. This is the awareness that we are meant to live our life, a place of pure energy where we feel the "infinite oneness" *flowing* and *moving* and *stirring* within us. This is the Heaven that Jesus wanted us to experience, an ever-present and expanding creative energy, which is within our grasp, if we turn to it and believe; it is an unseen miracle before your eyes.

Emilie Cady writes in her book, *How I Used Truth*, "There is but one hand in the universe. It is God's hand. Whenever you have felt that your hand was empty, it has been because you have believed yourself separate from God. Where do you suppose comes the desire to give of yourself? Is it from the mortal part of you? No, it is the voice of the Giver of all good gifts crying out through you ... your hand is God's hand. My hand is God's hand. Our Father reaches out through these, His only hands." To be in the Spirit is to realize at the depth of your being that you are the hands, the feet, the arms, the heart of God in expression, that you are one with this life, this energy. As St. Francis said, "to be the instrument of God's love in this world."[26]

To move through these layers of awareness is not as simple as the wave of the hand and presto, magically, we are there. Although, at times, we might find ourselves "there" quite by accident for a short time; once there, it is the only place we want to live; we want to be there all the time. How do we get there? Awareness is the first step. We have to be aware that this layer/level of awareness exists, and that it is what Jesus and the other spiritual masters have encouraged us to achieve. Then we need to discipline ourselves to follow the guide that Jesus left us: Practice the ways of love and forgiveness, non-resistance, detachment and non-judgment; be the attitude of your conscious choosing; and direct your every good thought toward that ever-expanding reality of good, which is looking for the light of the infinite to fill your being. We will create a *ripple* in a layer of our consciousness that will take us to a new level of being. We begin to *see* the universe working a little differently. We shall indeed "know" that the Kingdom of Heaven is like an onion, comprised of many different and unique layers of awareness.

I am open to the fullness of life!

---

26 Lesson's in Truth, Emilie Cady, Unity Books, Unity Village Missouri

Resources for this chapter

- Notes of lecture given by The Reverend Michael Beckwith

- The Interpreter's One-Volume Commentary on the Bible, Abingdon Press, Nashville, TN, page 1106

- Revelation the Road to Overcoming, Charles Neal, Unity Books, Unity Village Missouri page *v*

- Bible Overview, Learners Workbook, Unity Institute, page 317

- Lesson's in Truth, Emilie Cady, Unity Books, Unity Village Missouri

- Sacred Myths, Marilyn McFarlane, Sibyl Publications, Portland Oregon

- The Holy Bible, New Revised Standard Version

River of Life

I trust that the River of Life knows where it is going,
so I let go and I allow Spirit to guide me!

A father and his five-year old son were headed for McDonald's one day, and passed a car accident. Usually, when they would see something terrible like that, they would say a prayer, so the dad pointed to the accident and said to his son, "We should pray." The boy bowed his head and said, "Please, God, do not let those cars block the entrance to McDonald's."

As a senior citizen was driving down the freeway, his car phone rang. Answering, he heard his wife's voice urgently warning him, "Herman, I just heard on the news that there is a car going the wrong way on Interstate 77. Please be careful!"

"Heck," Herman replied, "It is not just one car. It is hundreds of them!"

Sometimes, as we travel down the river of life, we miss the mark of what others are trying to tell us; sometimes, we do not even realize that we are moving against the flow, struggling to maintain our position. We need to trust that the current knows where it is going and the river of life delights to lift us free, if only we dare to let go.

There is an old saying: "There are only two things for sure in life, death and taxes." I am sure you have heard it. Clever cliché, but I do not buy it! Do you? Taxes are pretty common in our modern society, especially here in Oklahoma, but if I went out to a South Sea island or exploring deep space, I would not have to pay taxes there, would I? Well, maybe. Death is something we all experience, at least physically, but I believe, that spiritually, life is eternal. Either way, that statement just never felt right. Life can be so much more than that rather pessimistic statement!

Several years ago, I watched the movie *Star Trek: Generations*. It was great. I love Star Trek and any kind of futuristic sci-fi movies. I always find something that speaks to my soul. In one scene, the arch-villain appears to be winning in the struggle of the destruction of a planet, and declares part of that age-old quote, "There is only one constant in the universe, and it is death." The irony of the scene is profound. I can see and feel life teeming all around them, and every fiber of my being wants to scream out, "No, there is one constant in the universe, and it is life!" As the scene progresses, Captain Jean Luc Picard, of the USS Enterprise, seems to read my mind and says, "No, my friend, the one constant in the universe is life."[27]

The one constant of the universe is life, and life is in a continual state of change and evolution, moving from one form into another. Just look around, and you will see change everywhere. Mother Nature fosters these changes through the weather, and the rotation of its seasons. In the fall, the trees lose their leaves and go dormant for the winter, while birds change their geographical location and fly south. Then, in spring, the trees and flowers bloom and the birds return. Caterpillars change into butterflies. There is a natural flow and a divine order in all life, and change is part of it. The cells in our bodies are continually cleansing and renewing themselves. There is a constant motion of change going on throughout our bodies. Scientists say every seven years we have literally replaced every cell in our body; we are made completely new from head to toe.

In his book, *The Power of Wisdom,* Aman Motwane acknowledges this reality very powerfully: "In nature, everything is dynamic—resonating, pulsating, oscillating, wiggling, and flitting. Every cell is continually growing, mutating, morphing. Every atom, every molecule, every planet is circling incessantly around its nucleus. The earth is hurtling through

---

27 Star Trek, Generations, The Movie, Paramount Pictures

space at 64,300 miles per hour."[28] We are all on this huge rock speeding across the universe, while it rotates every twenty-four hours, while circling a tremendous burning ball of gas. Can you feel the wind blowing in your face? Can you imagine a bigger amusement park ride? Yet, the vast majority of us are unaware of the speeds we are traveling, silently wondering why we cannot bring order and stability to the chaos we perceive in the world. We are really out of touch with reality!

The human mind so wants to bring order to the chaos it perceives. Our minds have a natural tendency to label, divide, and describe everything, trying to bring order to it, so we might understand it and bring it under our dominion. We tame wild animals and bring them into our cities and our homes. We study the weather and seek to predict its patterns and ultimately control it, so it might be more productive and less destructive. We try to gain a sense of order by putting things into clearly marked areas and categories. We write laws, policies, and procedures to define acceptable and unacceptable behavior. We form groups, organizations, and nations. We develop maps, directories, programs, and instructions on how to sift through, organize, package, and label this chaos of information, which always seems to be changing.

All of this helps us give some sense of order, so we can function. Everything has to have its place and fit into our logically oriented universe. It is vital to our survival, at least psychologically. Unfortunately, one person's order is often another person's chaos. For example, do you organize your stuff in horizontal files or vertical stacks? My wife organizes by creating vertical stacks and I am forever looking for things. Likewise, she seldom finds anything I have filed horizontally.

Most people take man-made borders, labels and organizations far too literally and rigidly; forgetting that boundaries and demarcations were created in someone's mind, to help us make sense and bring some type of order to our ever-evolving world. However, these organizational structures and borders, which we have created, have no basis in reality. Nature does not share our need to create boundaries. Nature does not care that we draw lines to separate California from Nevada, or the United States from Mexico, or Iraq from Iran. In nature, there is no fixed line of

---

28 *The Power of Wisdom*, Aman Motwane, Prakash Press, Redondo Beach CA

separation between the ocean and the sand, the hills and the valleys, or the tree from its roots. When a storm rolls in, it does not stop and ask the local authorities which way would be the best to proceed.

We label and organize and structure, but still, there are times our world seems to be spinning out of our control. We steadfastly cling to anything that appears remotely predictable and stable. Just about the time, we think we have figured it all out, everything changes. We are pulled in many different directions, torn between family and career, our wants and our needs. We measure them against what is considered to be *right and wrong*. Consequently, our search for stability and order remains quite elusive, because in nature there is not a perfect state of being without change. The universe is in constant motion, always changing and evolving. In nature, equilibrium and stability do not come from being in a perfect unchanging state; they come from finding the resonance and harmony in any given situation, from finding the ideal flow in the river of life.

Think of how a pendulum in one of those big museums swings back and forth, and back and forth, without ever standing quite still. It flirts continually with the ideal perfect position, where it would be completely vertical and in balance, but it never actually comes to rest at any one position. This is the natural order of things. This is the way things are. The illusion of a *perfect world* —a balanced unchanging world—is simply a wish, a projection of man's mortal mind onto our world.

The constant swirling, twirling and circling of life appears to be the source of uncertainty, but in actuality, it can be the root of all certainty. There is rhythm in the movement of the river of life. It is how nature choreographs everything and gets things done. This includes our own body, which appears to be stable enough, but even it is in a constant state of movement. Our heart within us beats, pulsates, and throbs incessantly, and, because it does, our body is able to move, walk, run, and jump (well at least some of the time). Our minds are able to think, reflect, imagine, and innovate. This rhythm is the energy of *life*.

In nature, order and stability do not come from being in a vacuum—a perfect unchanging constant state—they come from getting in the rhythm of the constantly changing, evolving, vibrating field of energy that surrounds us. Deep down, I believe that this is why people love doing those extreme sports like surfing, mountain climbing, racing motorcycles, and sky diving; they can feel the pulse of the universe when they find the rhythm of whatever they are doing.

Although we are often unaware of it, there is a rhythm inherent in the energies of life, and we can consciously observe it. When we do, we see that nothing stops resonating. Even things that appear to be solid, like our body; when looked at under a microscope, we see that they are constantly vibrating and moving. The vibrating, changing, moving character of this field of energy is the very essence of life. What would happen if all this activity just stopped? Everything would cease to exist; it would all collapse in upon itself.

When we truly understand this very basic truth of our reality, the way we perceive life completely changes. Our need to bring a sense of structure and order to the chaos we perceive in the world simply falls away. We stop striving to acquire things for our physical security, seek to get into the rhythm of the universe, and to see things as they really are. Just as Jesus advised: "Seek first the Kingdom of God and Its harmony and all things you desire will be yours as well" (Mathew 6:33 NRSV and Aramaic Translations). As we align ourselves with the harmony of the Kingdom, our compulsion to set things right evaporates, our struggle to control vanishes. This, in itself, reduces the commotion in our life exponentially. Once we stop struggling with the currents of the river of life, and let things be, as they have to be, we remove the biggest source of agitation: ourselves.

It is kind of like downhill skiing. I love skiing. I learned to ski when I was much younger and a little crazy. When most people first learn to ski, they buy into the illusion of the mountain, the snow and the ice, which can be intimidating. It is natural to give in to the fear of falling and hurting yourself, so we are naturally off balance. We crouch, bend, tighten up, and resist the harmony and flow that is inherent in skiing. It is really hard to ski this way.

I learned to ski quite by accident. The first time I went skiing, I went with a bunch of my college buddies, who also had never been skiing before. I guess that was our first mistake. We did not know what any of those signs meant. So, the first time up we got on the wrong chair lift and went straight to the top of the mountain. To our surprise, we discovered the only way down was for experts only. Oops!

After falling five times in the first 20 yards, I decided just to stand up straight, relax and stay in line with the hill; which is a pretty crazy thing to do for a beginner. You see, I somehow instinctively knew to align myself with the natural downhill pull of the slope, and I let go. I found there was a beautiful rhythm as I surrendered my need to control my direction, as I went hurling down the slope. I do not know why I did not fall. The strangest thing is, the faster you go the more balance and harmony you feel. Do you know what happens if you stop moving while you are on the slope of the mountain? It is just like when you stop moving on a bicycle; you fall over. Well, let me say, I was really glad I was in the foothills of Virginia and not on one of those real mountains in Colorad0!

Since that first experience, many years ago, I learned it is the *character* of a ski slope to pull you down the hill along the line of gravity, called the "fall line." If you ski straight down this fall line, you will speed down the mountain in a real hurry, and that can be a really exhilarating experience—or NOT! Perhaps, you are one of those skiers who want to resist the character of the slope, by crouching and bending over. Like I said, this really is not a fun way to ski. You find that you do not get very far very quickly, or you fall a lot, because you are resisting and fighting the natural pull of the slope and you are unable to establish any type of balance.

I have learned that, if I can find the natural flow of the slope, I can use it as a way to balance myself as I traverse the hill in a wonderful harmony, always looking ahead of my own line of travel to see what lies ahead. I learned that, when I find the rhythm of the mountain, I could do many neat things: like a "Back Scratchier," or a "Helicopter," or jump from the top of one mogul to the next. I learned to get into the flow of the rhythm of the mountain.

The truth is, all of life has a natural flow and rhythm inherent within it. Remember, the earth is traveling 64, 300 miles per hour across the universe, while beneath our feet it revolves and rotates incessantly, and because it does, the seasons change, and animals and plant-life thrives. Everything in nature has a scintillating rhythm, and this rhythm is the cause of everything. It sets the tone and pace for everything that happens. It is the source of nature's momentum. It is the natural character—*the righteousness*—of God's Kingdom. When we learn to look for and recognize this innate movement within life, we find a key that unlocks the doors of the Kingdom. We learn to stop fighting against the forces of nature and look for the patterns, and we seek to get into flow of the river of life, as opposed to struggling to control its current.

It is like riding down a stream in a canoe on a beautiful spring morning. You can feel the harmony of nature all around you. Your heart and soul are serene and at peace. Birds' chirp and soar in the sky. Ahead, a family of deer drinks from the stream. Beauty is everywhere. Then your eye catches a beautiful flower at the end of a branch that reaches out over the stream. You stand up and reach for the flower, but you only get the branch. As you struggle to reach the flower to look at it more closely, you feel a great surge in the canoe, and it begins to fill with water. Your struggle continues until you are about to fall in the water, and then you hear a voice call out, "Let Go!"

You can continue to struggle to look at that one beautiful flower, and in all likelihood fall in, or you can let go, and gently float down the stream to take in the beauty just around the corner.

Sounds so simple, yet we all cling to those beautiful flowers we want to keep. We hold onto many things that we were meant to experience for only a short time. If we let go of the branch, the turbulence ends.

Letting go is the real challenge in life. Letting go of the need to control and make things in our own image. Letting go of the fear of what we might lose when we release the things we cherish. We never realize that unless we release the images of the things we have held onto in the past, we are not open to the things that come our way in the present. Change is inevitable; it is part of the rhythm of life. How well we adapt to change, determines how successful we are in life. If we view our lives from this broader perspective, we learn to see that each episode along the way, no matter how difficult at the time, proves to be a stepping-stone to a greater good. It is all part of the divine flow of the river of life, every twist and turn leads in to a deeper and deeper awareness of the Infinite One's presence.

The next time everything seems to be going wrong, and you feel confused and at your wit's end, do not kick and wail and splash in the river of life; rather, still your mind and seek the Kingdom of God and its harmony. Spirit beckons to us from deep within, "Trust that the current knows where it is going and that the river of life delights to lift you free," if only you dare let go and let God. Life is an incredible journey; so enjoy the ride on the ever-changing river of life.

I trust that the River of Life knows where it is going,
so I let go and I allow Spirit to guide me

Resources for this talk:

- <u>Star Trek, Generations,</u> The Movie, Paramount Pictures

- <u>Illusions, The Adventures of a Reluctant Messiah,</u> Richard Bach,
  Dell Publishing Co, & New York

- <u>The Power of Wisdom,</u> Aman Motwane, Prakash Press Redondo Beach CA.

- <u>The Prayers of the Cosmos,</u> Neil Douglas-Koltz, Harper
  and Row Publisher San Francisco, & New York

- <u>The Quest, A Journey of Spiritual Rediscovery,</u> Richard and
  Mary Alice Jafolla Unity Books, Unity Village MO.

- <u>The Holy Bible,</u> *NRSV and Aramaic Translations*

- Opening Jokes, www.positivechristianity.org, Rev. Christopher Chenowenthe,
  founder.

Five Simple Tools

Spirit dreams through me and I give expression to it.

An older couple was lying in bed one morning. They had just awakened from a good night's sleep. The husband reached over to take his wife's hand but she cried out, "Don't touch me."

"Why not?" he asked.

She answered, "Because I'm dead."

The husband, not quiet believing the conversation, asked, "What are you talking about? We're both lying here in bed together and talking to one another!"

"Oh no," she said, "I'm definitely dead."

He exclaimed, "You're not dead! What in the world makes you say you're dead?" She replied, "Because, when I woke up this morning nothing hurt."

It is odd what some people become attached to. I can really relate to this joke. There have been mornings when I wake up and every part of my body is hurting. I remember one of those particularly cold winter weeks in Oklahoma, when we got one of our famous ice storms. The storm provided a mixture of freezing rain and ice blended all together. During most of the storm, it was coming down in little pellets of snow like a snowmaking machine makes on a ski slope. The storm mixture covered everything with a sheet of ice three to four inches deep. On the days following the storm, I would wake up each morning with my hands and legs hurting, from chipping ice and compacted snow off the sidewalks around the church and at home. This ice mixture was really hard stuff. The snow shovel I was used to using would not even make a dent in it.

At one point, I realized if I was going to make any progress at all in clearing a safe path on the sidewalk, I would need a special tool: a straight-edged shovel. When I found that straight-edged shovel, and used it, I succeeded in making cracks in the ice, here and there. Finally, I was able to make a hole all the way down to the sidewalk. Then I left it and allowed the natural forces of nature—the sun and the temperature—go to work. When I came back later, I found that not only had the hole widened a little but also there was sliver of space under the ice, which allowed me to use the straight-edged shovel more effectively. I would force the tool underneath the layer of ice and was able to break it into sheets of ice, one or two feet long, making my shoveling chore a whole lot easier. In some places on the north side of the building, I broke off pieces of ice I could barely lift.

Splintering the ice into big pieces made the work go quickly, and left no residual ice sticking to the sidewalk. I was really glad I had discovered that simple tool and a technique to help me. Whenever I found a spot too difficult to clear, I just made a little crack in the top of the ice, let the natural forces of nature go to work on it, and came back when the time was right to pry the long blocks of ice loose with that simple tool.

Likewise, I have found that utilizing five simple tools on my spiritual path has helped to chip through the ice and clay of my mortal mind, so that I might experience what lies hidden beneath my sometimes-frosty exterior. Yes—that's right five simple tools have helped me to break through the ice, and hard outer shell of the mortal mind, just like that straight-edged shovel helped me to break through the hard outer shell of ice that covered our sidewalks. The five simple tools I have used on my spiritual journey have not only helped me to sense, feel, and know the richness of Spirit in myself, but they have helped me to see and feel Spirit's Presence in others. These five simple tools are relatively easy to understand, but not always so easy to remember when we find ourselves getting caught up in one of life's little situations. It is kind of like chipping ice away from the sidewalk; you have to use them with the right technique, and you have to be very persistent.

I have discussed the use of these tools in a variety of places throughout this book, but perhaps not quite so succinctly as I will here. Nor have I discussed them together as system or a discipline for your spiritual journey. The basis for these five simple tools, as a spiritual discipline, can be found in numerous books on spirituality, especially in the Bible. Jesus talks about all five tools during the Sermon on the Mount, which is recorded in chapters five, six, and seven of the Gospel of Matthew and in chapters eleven and twelve of the Gospel of Luke. If you are familiar with these five simple tools, just use this chapter as a reminder to use them on a daily basis. It might help you avoid some of those challenges by which you periodically find yourself confronted. What are these five simple tools?

The first tool is one I am sure everyone has heard of. It is called the **Law of Mind Action**—you know, that thoughts held in mind produce after their kind. Like fertile soil, the creative power of the mind does not differentiate between the seed of the weed or that of a flower, it simply responds to the seed thought and puts its energy behind into manifesting the idea in mind. It is very important to become conscious of the thoughts we hold in our minds and to focus our attention on what we want, instead of the things we do not want. The metaphysical movie *The Secret* calls this tool the Law of Attraction. *The Secret* discusses a whole variety of ways that the Law of Mind Action is engaged and plays out in our life. Jesus said it this way: "According to your faith it will be done onto you." "Ask and you shall receive." "All things are possible, if you believe."

Since the Law of Mind Action is the focus of a number of the stories I have shared with you (my house on West Hutchinson, and my Explorer are good examples), and since it is a frequently discussed topic of new thought Christianity, I will not say more.

The second tool needed, to keep our path clear on our journey, is also very familiar; it is called **forgiveness.** Chances are, if you asked someone what Jesus taught their response would be, "Love and Forgiveness." Despite the importance that Jesus placed on this tool, many people have a hard time with forgiveness. Perhaps that is because they misunderstand the purpose of forgiveness and try using it in an upside-down manner. If you were to use the opposite end of the straight-edged shovel to crack ice, how successful do you think you would be? You might even break the shovel and hurt yourself in the process. However, that is the way many people try using the tool of forgiveness. Most people believe that forgiveness is for the other guy—to let them off the hook for something they did wrong; after all, we all want justice to be done. I was right, and they were wrong and I am going to make them pay. Forgiveness will never work with that type of mindset.

You see forgiveness is not for the other guy; it is for us. It is to release the pain and the hurt from within us. As long as we are holding onto resentment or judgment, we will never be set free from the experience, nor will we know the fullness of love or the goodness of life. Jesus pretty much said this when he said, "If you are angry with your brother or sister, you will be liable to judgment and if you cuss or use profanity towards them, you will be liable to the council, or if you say "You Fool" you will be liable to the fires of Gahanna." Now, I am sure you have never said any so extreme!

Jesus goes on to say, "Come to terms with your adversary, while you are on the way to find justice, because you are the one who will be held prisoner, and you will not get out until you have paid the last pence" (Matthew 5:22-26). The word "forgive" literally means to give forth. It allows us to release and let go of all that holds us in bondage. Forgiveness helps to first create cracks in those beliefs that no longer serve us, then helps to remove the barriers in our minds that block us from our good. Forgiveness is a process. This is why when one of the disciples asked Jesus how often he should persist in the practice of forgiveness, Jesus replied, "You must forgive seventy times seven."

Now if you do not like practicing forgiveness, the last three tools are for you. If you practice using these tools, you will never have to worry about forgiveness again, because there will be nothing for you to release. You will find perfect peace, harmony and love in all you do. Does that not sound like a great deal? If you are interested, keep reading.

Do you remember the one thing Jehovah told Adam not to do, in that garden story in the book of Genesis? He said, "Don't eat from fruit of the Tree of the Knowledge of Good and Evil," because it will make you really sick! "Surely in the day that you eat of it you shall die!" Do you think Adam and Eve, being just a couple of days old, understood what Jehovah was trying to tell them? I mean kids will be kids! If you tell a child not to do something, what is the first thing they do? They test their limits. Adam and Eve were no different. You might think that an all-knowing God would have known better than to put such tasty-looking treats in plain sight—if he really did not want them to eat the fruit. When Adam and Eve ate that delicious looking fruit at the center of the garden, did they die?

No, they did not die a physical death—although they did experience a type of death—but in eating the fruits of the Tree of Knowledge of Good and Evil, they believed they had been separated from God's Presence and the sense of oneness they had found in the garden. Likewise, each time we bite into the fruit of the Tree of the Knowledge of Good and Evil, we die a little bit, to the good in our life and to Spirit's Presence, until there comes a point where all we can see is darkness and despair.

Remember Jesus' warning us: "Judge not, for with what judgment you judge, you shall be judged ..." (Matthew 7:1 – 2). Why do you think he said that? Many people fall into the trap called judgment (forgetting this core concept in Jesus' teachings), perhaps to gain power, to control, or to instill fear in someone else. One thing we do know is that judging things is one of our most basic tendencies, and something that creates a great deal of trouble for us. When we bite into duality, we separate ourselves from the awareness of Spirit's Presence. We believe that we must choose between these two opposites—good or evil – it is your choice. When, in fact, there is only one presence and one power in the universe and that is God the good!

Everything that we perceive as sin and evil arises out of this sense of separation. What we perceive as sin and evil does not originate in Divine Mind; it exists because humankind persists in thinking and believing in separation and in the ways of judgment and darkness. From this sense of separation, we choose to identify with negative emotions and concepts of ourselves, which are lies and illusions. The result is a sin; that is we have missed the mark of our highest potential and of our truest self.

Remember Jesus advised, from the Sermon on the Mount, "In all things let your speech be yea, yea or nea, nea, everything else comes from the evil one." (Matthew 5:37) Which I have come to believe, Jesus was referring to the darkness of our own ego mind. Whenever you bump into one of those experiences you do not like, just say, "This is not for me; I must be on my way." Then allow that to be okay. What normally happens, when we find ourselves in a situation we do not like, is that our ego gets involved and we want people to see it our way.

When we practice the tool of **non-judgment**, it empowers us to see clearly to the heart of the every situation, without the hindrance of labeling something good or bad, right or wrong. It also allows us to be in any type of situation with an open heart, which helps us to reestablish our connection with the divine, and empowers us to see Spirit at work. When we learn not to bite into the fruits of the Tree of Knowledge of Good and Evil, through the discipline of non-judgment, we realize that we are still in the garden and that God has never left our side.

Now let us move on to the fourth tool needed to embrace the spiritual journey. I would like you to think about the one thing in your life that is most important to you, be it a possession, a relationship or an idea. What is that one thing that is more important than anything else in the world? Can you visualize it, and hold that vision in your heart, and think about how good it is? Well, it has no value whatsoever! That is right; it has no value! How does that make you feel? Angry, lost, bewildered? Good. Joel Goldsmith writes in his book, *Living Between Two Worlds*, "The human being lives in a world of material sense; this means that he measures life in terms of amounts, weights, degrees ... and rights and wrongs ... He ascribes powers of good to some individuals and powers of evil to other individuals. He is always conferring and labeling power upon someone or something. His entire human experience is made up of a combination of good and evil, giving power to all kinds of things external to himself ... He is either the beneficiary or the victim. Rarely does he acknowledge that he has dominion and lives from this dominion."[29]

In the second chapter of Genesis, Jehovah showed Adam around the garden, and told him he had the power to name everything that came into his existence; that he had dominion over the material realm. Likewise, you have been given dominion over everything that comes into your life; you have been given the power to name and label everything. The only reason why certain things have a place of importance in your life is because you have said so. You have given them power in your life, power

---

29 <u>Living Between Two World,</u> Joel S. Goldsmith, I-Level Publications Publishers, Austell, GA, page 54

to control your state of mind and your moods. When you allow things outside of yourself to determine how you feel or how you react, you have given your power away to those things.

This was the reason Jesus related the precept of the camel going through the eye of the needle to that rich young man (Matthew 19). He was not saying that rich people could not experience eternal life, but rather that people who have attachments to possessions, to relationships, to concepts, and to beliefs must be willing to let those things go, or they will not be able to experience the Kingdom. When they are able to let go of these attachments, they will see and experience those things they love and prize from a whole new reality; seeing things without personal attachment opens us to seeing things through the eyes of Spirit. However, if we are unwilling to let go of our own preconceived ideas, opinions, and emotional attachments, we falter on our path. Since the beginning of time, we have had dominion over all things that come into our lives. You have the power to name and label everything in your life; how have you labeled them? The tool of **detachment** can be a very powerful tool in our life. Like that lady in the opening story, who gave her power away to the pain she felt; by holding on tightly to our attachments, we limit the good we are able to experience each day.

The **Art of Nonresistance** is the final spiritual tool I would like to discuss. It is probably the least understood, and least practiced, of all disciplines, because it is counter to human nature, especially in the 21st century. When someone, or something, pushes against us, it is our natural tendency to push back. However, when we push back, we often get caught in the force that pushed against us; the harder we struggle to escape, the more we become tangled in its web. Noting this phenomenon of human behavior, the great psychologist Carl Jung said, "What you resist persists."

I believe this is why Jesus said, "Resist not an evildoer. If anyone strikes you on the cheek, offer him the other … I say to you love your enemies and pray for those who persecute you" (Matthew 5:38-43). Wisdom for a lifetime! Unfortunately, these words are rarely heeded; especially by those who proclaim to follow in Jesus' footsteps. Jesus often repeated the phrase, "In all things, seek first the Kingdom of God and Its harmony and balance" (The Aramaic word for harmony and balance was translated as righteousness). When we become nonresistant to the various forces that push against us, we look past the appearances of any circumstances, and seek the harmony of the Kingdom. Consequently, those negative or overbearing influences just pass through us, and we are not pulled into the web of those who would lead us down a path we do not want to travel. When we seek only the Kingdom of Heaven and its harmony, that is what we find; thus we are not pulled into the illusion of duality.

Five simple tools for the spiritual journey: the Law of Mind Action, forgiveness, non-judgment, detachment, and non-resistance. Easy to understand, but not always so easy to remember and apply when we find ourselves getting caught up in life's little situations. However, when we can learn to apply them, we find a way to chip through the ice and clay of the mortal mind, thereby uncovering what lies hidden deep beneath its cold exterior. We discover our true self, and the way to experience Heaven on earth.

Spirit dreams through me and I give expression to it

Resources for this chapter

- <u>Discover the Power Within You</u>, Eric Butterworth, Harper Collins, New York, NY

- <u>Living Between Two World</u>, Joel S. Goldsmith, I-Level Publications Publishers, Austell, GA

- <u>The Prayers of the Cosmos</u>, Neil Douglas-Koltz, Harper and Row Publisher San Francisco, New York NY

- <u>The Holy Bible, New Revised Standard Version</u>

The Kingdom of Heaven is Like a Kite

I allow the breath of the Infinite to take me to new heights.

Once, there was a kite that soared high in the skies, high above the others, but it was a very unhappy kite. The kite cried out, "If I just didn't have this heavy tail pulling against me all the time, I just know I could rise higher and higher up into the sky. Oh, I hope someday I can shake this tail loose." However, try as it might, that kite could not get free from its tail. So, it continued to fly ... and complain.

However, one day a particularly strong wind came and blew the tail off. What a wonderful sensation! Free at last! Free at last! The kite soared for a few moments to a great height. And then ... it plunged downward and crashed into the ground. Poor kite! It did not know that, without the combination of the upward push of the wind in its sails and the downward pull from the weight of its tail, a kite would not be able to fly at all.

When I was a teenager, I would go to the Battlefields of Manassas and watch hundreds of people flying kites. It was a spacious park, with mostly cleared land that stretched for miles; there were no telephone poles or wires to tangle a kite. The kites filled the air and soared over the landscape. Some kites would sail high above all the others, gracefully dancing in the wind. They were the ones that had the longest and heaviest tails. To me this always seemed to defy logic. How could they fly with all that weight?

As strange as it might seem, the Kingdom of Heaven is like a kite. Now I want to assure you this was not something that Jesus said. No, Jesus never said that! I do not believe they had such technology in his time. However, if they did, I am sure that he would have used the analogy. Why? Because he used many other everyday life occurrences to explain and illustrate how the Kingdom of Heaven is an ever-present reality. This analogy just seems to fit really well. How? Why would I say that the Kingdom of Heaven is like a kite?

For me, Heaven is the realization that the breath of the Infinite One fills my lungs with life, inspires my mind with creative ideas, and guides me in the ways of love and peace. In other words, if I were a kite, it would be the Holy Spirit filling my sails. But were it not for the steadiness and discipline I have gained in meeting life's challenges, I would only catch the updraft of the breath of Spirit for a moment, before I would plunge downward and crash into the earth. Actually, this is one of the challenges for those who are new to the spiritual path. It can seem like a roller coaster of ups and downs. I am sure this can be fun if you understand that you will be riding the roller coaster, as you're developing your spiritual understanding and discipline. Steadiness in life is found only through daily discipline (prayer, meditation, and using the five simple tools). Your spiritual discipline is the tail that provides weight for your journey in life, and allows the breath of the infinite to lift you higher and higher.

However, like the kite that tried to shake loose of its tail, we often whine and complain about the challenges and burdens that come our way. We allow them to overwhelm us, instead of seeing the opportunity within them. The challenges, obstacles, and those very special people we meet along the way—you know the ones I'm talking about—are opportunities for us to hone and develop our spiritual discipline. What if we could make that shift in awareness the moment we experienced a challenge? What if we stopped resisting the challenge and relied on our inner discipline? What would your life be like? How high could Spirit lift you before you began to wobble and became dizzied by new heights?

The other day I realized I was like Albert Einstein! You know my wife laughed when I told her that (probably in just the same way you are laughing now). She said, "Well, there are times your hair is really messy and sticks up in the air." Now, Albert was really intelligent. I am not implying that I am all that! But often, he would have many different thoughts running through his head at one time. Often he would be unable to finish a complete sentence, before his mind went off to another thought.

That is really how I am like him. This habit does tend to make some people a little crazy. Well, the other day, I learned that Albert and I had something else in common: dyslexia. Dyslexia is a learning disorder. The first time I heard that Albert Einstein had dyslexia, I thought, *"Albert Einstein had a learning disorder?"*

Dyslexia is a condition in which the mind sees things differently from the norm, often flip-flopping letters, words, objects, and concepts. Through special training, lots of practice, and determination I have learned to read, write, and focus my mind like everyone else. Well, most of the time. When I begin talking really fast, or when I am excited, I have tendency to say things backwards. I am not talking in a code or speaking in tongues—at least, I do not think so.

As I have mentioned before, dyslexia has created much havoc in my life—especially before I learned about dyslexia, while taking an early childhood development class in college, and realized that it had been the cause of many of the problems I had experienced while in grade school. It explained so much to me. It was why I had those bizarre difficulties, like always making certain numbers backwards. My teachers would get so mad at me. It explained why I would often get questions wrong, when I knew the answers. It explained why I struggled with English and had little fondness for reading.

As a result of my dyslexia, I experienced challenges that perhaps I might not have otherwise, such as my huge fear of public speaking. The idea of standing before people and speaking sent me into a panic. However, when I learned that I had that dyslexia, I was twenty-two years old and at the end of my formal educational experience, so I thought that would be the end of the problems I experienced as a result of dyslexia. At least that is what I thought. However, issues revolving around my dyslexia began showing up in my work place. I told myself I would just have to learn to adjust, to focus more, to try harder, to learn more by pure memory, and to learn to work faster than anyone else to make up for the mistakes I was sure to make. For me, it was one of those burdens that I have wished, and wished I could be free of. I pleaded, "Lord please take this burden from me, so that I might be able to fly higher."

Then, something happened. I cannot really remember when, perhaps it was after coming to Oklahoma City. Perhaps it was just one of those gradual awakenings. I began to realize all the ways that dyslexia had actually benefited me. Sure, it created challenges, but those challenges have only made me more understanding and stronger. It has also given me gifts that other people simply do not possess. It has given me the ability to see outside the box, because I see a completely different box. It has given me the capacity to see that there are many different ways of doing a particular thing.

Most of all, dyslexia has taught me, after much practice and discipline, that if something does not look right or feel right, it probably is not right, and there is a different way of looking at it. When I feel that something is out of place, I stop, take a deep breath in, and ask for guidance. Dyslexia has also taught me to ask for help with the things I simply do not do well, which is something I would never have done before.

As Aman Motwane would say, "There are two sides to every coin."[30] I began to see the flip side of dyslexia. It was then that my resistance to dyslexia, and the heartache I experienced over it, dissolved.

Can you see the blessing hidden in the burdens, or challenges, that lie before you? If you can, you will be able to tie more and more lengths onto the tail called discipline, so that you will soar higher and higher on the breath of Spirit. You might recall that dyslexia has not been my only challenge. There was Terry Brown, one of my former bosses who was called "Hitler's evil twin" by his employees. There were my core issues regarding my feelings of unworthiness. Let's just say that I have had a number of challenges and personal growth issues to deal with. However, as I began to apply spiritual discipline to each of those old patterns and beliefs, they lost their power and influence over me, and I was freed to focus on the many blessings that surrounded me, and on the potential that lies before me.

Jesus was asked repeatedly when the Kingdom would come. I can see Jesus looking up to the skies, and saying, "Oy Vey, Father aren't they ever

---

30 During a workshop with Aman Motwane *on his book the Power of Wisdom,* Prakash Press, Redondo Beach CA.

going to get it?" Then responding, "The Kingdom of God is not coming with things that can be observed; nor will they say, 'Look, here it is!' or 'There it is!' For, in fact, the Kingdom of Heaven is in the midst of you" (Luke 17:20). The Kingdom of God, Heaven, the Divine Oneness ... it is in the midst of us—you and me. It is the field of life, the creative energy that surrounds and enfolds us. The Kingdom is not to be observed in our external experience, because we are, in fact, in the midst of the invisible realm of Spirit. We are part of it. The Breath of the Infinite fills our lungs with life, inspires our mind with creative ideas, and guides us in its ways.

As Jesus said, "The Father who dwells in me does this work. Believe me that I am in the Father and the Father is in me" (John 14:10 –11). Before we can come into this truer, deeper understanding of our relationship with the Infinite, we need to be able to move through the fears and the beliefs that hold us back and restrict us. To soar to the heights of the spiritual dimension, we must deepen our awareness of the Breath of the Infinite, and hone the art of our spiritual discipline, so that we can realize that the challenges that lie before us are actually opportunities that will reveal hidden blessings.

Do you think an eagle worries or debates or questions where the Kingdom of Heaven is? I have a real fascination for eagles. One of my coworkers in the courier business in Chicago, knowing my fondest for eagles, would say, "It is hard to fly like an eagle when you are surrounded by turkeys." "If you don't want to be surrounded by turkeys don't work at the turkey farm." I guess he had a good opinion of the place we worked.

When we lived in Chicago, Yvonne and I would go skiing in the hills of Wisconsin. Driving up, we would stop in a small town along the Wisconsin River. The river has a series of turbulent rapids on the edge of the city—the only place for miles where the river was not frozen solid. The eagles would come down from the nesting grounds in the surrounding hills, and sit in the snow-covered trees beside the rapids, so they could go fishing for dinner in the churning water. The eagles would sit in the trees until they saw something stirring, and then stretch out their wings. With a few broad strokes, they would be soaring in the sky. Circling over the icy water until the time was just right, the eagles would dive into the river and come out with large fish. It was amazing! Every time they would dive, they would come up with a meal. They never missed.

Yes, eagles fascinate me. I have collected many inspirational writings and pictures of eagles, like the two in the lobby of my church. One is titled, *The Eagle's Story.*

"

"An eagle will soar effortlessly into storms, letting the wind carry him while other birds beat their wings frantically to stay aloft. He knows where there is safety in the storm. He knows that there are currents within the storm that will lift him higher and up out of the turbulence found at lower altitudes. From this higher altitude, he can see the storm more clearly, sensing its direction, and he knows what to do."

"At times an eagle must retire to shelter for renewal. There he will stretch out his soiled wings and extract the debris, which has collected and weighted him down, restricting his flight. Then he rests, later emerging in a renewed condition, stronger than before. With faith the eagle will stretch out its wings, and with a few majestic strokes take flight."

"When an eaglet is ready, its mother will soar high carrying the eaglet on her back, suddenly she will swoop and let it fall. Instinctively the young eagle will fly. Listening to an intuitive knowing, it stretches out its wings and flies like an eagle. After all, that is what it is. The eaglet knows its purpose and follows it's calling to soar higher."

"

Perhaps that is why we humans are so fascinated by these magnificent creatures; they know their purpose and their spiritual discipline, so to speak. I have watched an eagle soar for hours, spellbound by its beauty, power, and grace—all the while thinking to myself, and sometimes saying out loud, "I wish I could fly like an eagle." Have you ever felt that way?

Do you know, we can fly like an eagle and soar like a kite? We simply have forgotten how. We have forgotten the truth of who we are. And who are you?

See, I told you, you have forgotten.

You are children of God, created in the image and likeness of God. What is God? God is Spirit, Love, the Breath of Life, and the Sacred Energy of our Being.

Well, perhaps we cannot fly through the skies like an eagle (not just yet anyway), but we can soar over the challenges and storms in our life. We can be lifted up to a higher level of awareness, by following and mastering certain spiritual disciplines. Instead of learning how to fly like an eagle, stretching forth our spiritual wings and taking flight, we have learned the ways of the world. Where there is opportunity and potential, we have learned to see lack and limitation and to react from our fear.

When the eaglet's mother takes him out for his first flying lesson, she does not warn him of all the things that could go wrong, all the things that he needs to watch out for, or all the things he cannot do. She takes him out at full speed and just drops him. The eaglet, never knowing fear nor doubt, stretches out his wings with faith. Instinctively, an eaglet knows how to fly. After all, he is an eagle. Releasing our fears and our doubts, we too can soar, by honing our spiritual discipline and stretching forth our spiritual wings.

The next time you want to cry out, "Lord why do I have this burden constantly harassing me?" Remember that the Kingdom of Heaven is like a kite. Stop resisting it and bless it for the opportunity to put your spiritual practice to work. In order for us to soar to new heights in life, we must be able to develop that long tail called spiritual discipline.

"I allow the breath of the Infinite to take me to new heights."

Resources for this chapter:

- The Power of Wisdom, Aman Motwane, Prakash Press, Redondo Beach CA.

- *The Eagle's Story,* the picture in my lobby, Unity Church of Oklahoma City

- The Holy Bible, New Revised Standard Version

CPSIA information can be obtained
at www.ICGtesting.com
Printed in the USA
FFOW03n1402191217
44081167-43351FF